Christian Atheist

Belonging without
Believing

Christian
Atheist

Belonging without
Believing

Brian Mountford

BOOKS

Winchester, UK
Washington, USA

First published by O-Books, 2011
O-Books is an imprint of John Hunt Publishing Ltd., Laurel House, Station Approach,
Alresford, Hants, SO24 9JH, UK
office1@o-books.net
www.o-books.com

For distributor details and how to order please visit the 'Ordering' section on our website.

ISBN: 978 1 84694 439 0

Design: Stuart Davies

Printed in the UK by CPI Antony Rowe
Printed in the USA by Offset Paperback Mfrs, Inc

We operate a distinctive and ethical publishing philosophy in all
areas of our business, from our global network of authors to
production and worldwide distribution.

CONTENTS

Acknowledgements

First I must thank those who were generous and candid enough to allow me to interview them. They are named in Chapter one.

Apart from the specific interviews conducted for this book my ideas have been shaped by many other conversations and for this I must acknowledge my current colleagues Craig D'Alton and Charlotte Bannister-Parker and former colleagues Jane Shaw, Giles Fraser and Harriet Harris. Also Annette Mountford, Charlotte Mountford, Zoe Green, Rita Carter, Keith Ward, Val Cunningham, Margaret Kean, Johannes Zacchuber, Anthony Hawley, Rosemary Hawley, Phil Davis, Bleddyn Davies, Christine Ziehmann, Jonathan Williams, Andrew Teal, Alice Kent, Jack Cook, and Caroline Sants; the Bishop of Oxford for pressing me to continue when other work overtook me; Donald and Julia Reece for their hospitality in France as I prepared the final draft; my publisher John Hunt for his encouragement and patience.

Although his name has become shorthand for the anti-Christian position, Richard Dawkins remains a friend with whom I enjoy many neighbourly conversations.

Christian Atheist

About a year ago I invited the writer Philip Pullman to take part in a public discussion on his religious views and writing. It was just at the time of the release of the film *The Golden Compass*, based on his book *Northern Lights*, and the religious right in America was already campaigning against it on the grounds that they thought it was anti-God and anti-religion, even though most of them had never seen it. Pullman began by declaring, 'I am a Christian Atheist; a Church of England Atheist; a Book of Common Prayer Atheist. You could add a King James Bible Atheist, if you want. All those things go deep for me; they formed me; that heritage is impossible to disentangle, like a piece of barbed wire fence embedded in the bark of a tree. I've absorbed the Church's rituals and enjoy its language, which I knew as a boy, and now that it's gone I miss it.'

The phrase *Christian Atheist* stayed with me because it seemed such a good description of all the people I know who value the cultural heritage of Christianity - its language, art, music, moral compass, sense of transcendence - without actually believing in God; or, at least without believing in God in a way that would satisfy Christian orthodoxy, particularly in the metaphysics department, and I use it now as a catch-all for a wide variety of questioning and sceptical, but usually affectionate, takes on Christianity. The trouble is it seems to beg for greater precision. When I told one academic colleague that I was using 'Christian Atheist' as the working title for a book, he seemed genuinely curious but became increasingly critical when I was unable to define to his satisfaction exactly what I meant by the term. Another colleague, from the music faculty, said he liked the idea, then asked, half tongue in cheek, 'where do I go if I want to join?' To which I had no answer. Later, surfing the web to find out whether there was an organisation of this type that could be joined, I was surprised to find 'Christian Atheism' on the BBC website as a category within a range of descriptions of religious positions, but listed under 'atheism.' (An abridged form of the BBC statement is shown below).

Non-realism (Christian Atheism)
- Christian Atheists want to remove what they see as the fairy tale elements of Christianity.
- They prefer to call this a non-realistic version of Christianity, rather than Christian atheism. They say that they do believe in God - but not in a fairy tale way.

Essentials of non-realistic Christianity
- Religion is about internal spiritual experiences, and that is all.
- There is no world other than the material world around us.
- There are no beings other than the living organisms on this planet or elsewhere in the universe.
- There is no objective being or thing called God that exists separately from the person believing in him.
- There is no 'ultimate reality' outside human minds either.
- "God" is the way human beings put 'spiritual' ideals into a poetic form that they are able to use and work with. "God" is simply a word that stands for our highest ideals.
- God-talk is a language tool that enables us to talk about our highest ideals and create meaning in our lives.
- Religious stories and texts are ways in which human beings set down and work out spiritual, ethical, and fundamental meanings in life.

Worship and prayer
- If there's no God out there, it might seem pointless to go to church, or to pray. Christian Atheists would disagree: Worship is a beneficial activity. Worship in a group is good

way for a community to:

- communicate with each other, share ideals and ideas, explore the meaning and purpose of their individual lives, and the life of their community
- Hymn-singing and prayer are powerful ways for individual human beings to explore the meaning and purpose of their lives.
- Liturgies - the ceremonies and rituals of the church - are a powerful way of acting out the ideas that give meaning to our lives.

Benefits of this form of belief - Those who believe like this claim many advantages for it:

- Humanity is forced to take responsibility for everything.
- Religion no longer has to try to explain many difficult issues that go with believing in supernatural things.
- Religion is no longer in opposition to scientific progress.
- Religion is an inherently democratic, rather than hierarchical activity - it's something that comes from humanity, not something forced on us by a powerful God.

This account centres on a 'non-realist' understanding of God and seems to be based on the 'Sea of Faith' movement, which can be accessed on line and advertises meetings in twenty-six British towns and cities.

But I am interested in a wider and more miscellaneous phenomenon, made up of the seekers and doubters, opinionated rationalists, religious romantics, disillusioned ex-Church of Englanders, church musicians, thinkers about the universe, and also those who dip their toes in and out of the Christian sea. When I saw Samuel Johnson described as 'that worried and everlapsing believer,' I thought he should also join the team. That of course is the reality amongst those who care – in and out of faith, up and down, often inconstant, and if constant perhaps psychologically flawed.

But isn't Christian Atheism an oxymoron, every Christian creed beginning with 'I believe in God'? I have thought so for most of my life, from the moment my mother made me kneel at my bedside and pray, 'God bless mummy and daddy,' through my ordination in St Paul's Cathedral (witnessed by proud parents and a Masonic uncle in pin stripe trousers and bowler hat), to a career in defending the Faith. Now it's impossible not to take seriously the blitzkrieg of secularism on traditional religious ideas and beliefs; and its counterblast, the blinkered backlash of intolerant fundamentalism.

What has happened? There's been a paradigm shift. Like the movement of tectonic plates, paradigm shifts build up pressure over a long period of time and then move suddenly with earth-shaking effect. This one started with the rationalism of the Enlightenment, shook with the tremors of Republican France and global communism, science, technology, two world wars, the information revolution and the consequent process of globalisation, and bounced up the Richter Scale in the decade of 9/11 and the 'God Delusion.' OK, it would be far too flattering to Richard Dawkins to suggest that, godlike, he presided over the climactic moment, but it was at the beginning of this twenty-first century that atheism has taken its place as an entirely unembarrassed intellectual and social norm.

When my mother poured all that Christian culture into my young mind, I wouldn't be at all surprised if she was working on the Jesuit principle, 'give me the child and I will give you the man.' What is true for individuals is also true for nations. Just as languages prospered not through their intrinsic merit but through who was in power (Latin with the Roman Empire, English with the British Empire), so religion has its political enforcers: Saudi, Israel, the Emperor Constantine, Queen Elizabeth I spring to mind. To live in these states requires/required conformity and acceptance of a particular religious paradigm. To step out of line was risky and potentially fatal.

Now, in much of Europe at least, things have changed. We have a multicultural society where a minority belong to a variety of different faiths, but vast tracts of the population know little or nothing of the religion that shaped our history. They'll be glad to take a holiday at Christmas and Easter even if they have never heard of the Wise Men or the crucifixion. This is indifference on a mega scale towards what is perceived as some sort of old hat, once thought important by fools in old-style coats. But while the masses are indifferent, many intellectuals are positively hostile. The following quote from the Independent newspaper (7 September 2009) is typical. The writer is concerned that the rise of fundamentalism, Islamic, Jewish and Christian, will make global co-operation more difficult.

'The existence of a supernatural being in the form of a god who can dish out punishment in the afterlife may have been an important force in the past that helped to keep societies together as co-operative entities – but not so in the future.'

In America, by contrast, God and religion are more popular. But there are big regional variations, with coastal California and New England showing a similar secularism to Europe, while in the South creationism, faith schools, and the Ten Commandments on courtroom walls remain hotly debated questions – 'Bible Belt' issues, in which race is still deeply embedded.

From my own point of view, having lived my life tuned in to the regular rhythm of worship and the yearly cycle of the Christian story, it can be hard to own up to, or even to recognise, the change. When I have a Sunday off, I'm shocked to find the shopping centre heaving with people at 10.30 in the morning. I thought they'd all be in church. Besides it was only twenty years ago these same streets were deserted on a Sunday because our 'Christian' state refused to allow Sunday trading. Many of us still in touch with religion have underestimated the reach of secularism and would be gobsmacked to discover how meaningless Christian doctrine is to the population as a whole. You see we spend a great deal of time, my friends and I, thrashing out what seems to us a believable, up-to-date Christianity. We call on the support of two hundred years of intelligent open-minded people doing the same thing, when questions like ours were also being asked. Back in 1800, Samuel Taylor Coleridge's refused to accept original sin, substitutionary atonement, or hell as essential to faith; in 1921 Hastings Rashdall asserted that Jesus did not claim divinity for himself, that Jesus did not have a pre-existence before his birth, and that the virgin birth itself is not implied by the idea of incarnation. We are encouraged that it was the Church of England that supported the decriminalisation of homosexual behaviour as early as 1954 and suicide in 1959 and puzzled why the Church has now turned more conservative and should find itself so much at odds with the ethics of a civilised society. But however reasonably and sensibly we re-interpret these basic Christian ideas, however much we take on board evolution, relativity, literary criticism, and modern philosophy the end product remains, for most people, a Christianity that they can't believe in, assuming they care enough to try. With the genie out of the bottle, it's impossible to squeeze it back in and modern questions are too many and too penetrating to force back into Christianity's traditional dogmatic framework.

But this doesn't mean that the Christian enterprise is dead in the water. Its genius has not been reduced to rubble by the tremors of science or philosophy or globalisation. But it is looked at differently. Not everyone thinks it necessary to accept the whole package: old doctrines that make little sense are jettisoned. Traditional views of God are seen as optional; on the whole the ethical vision remains. The Church as an institution also has had a rough ride being rejected by many as corrupt, doctrinaire, hypocritical, repressive, and self-regarding. Or just plain dull. Can old style adherents cope with this?

So I decided to seek out some of these Christian Atheists and to ask them to tell me their stories. When the news got out, I soon found a queue at my door of people willing to spill the beans. Some I had only ever known in a secular context; others were members of my congregation. What had happened was that my first two subjects, business man Nigel Hamway and philosopher Roger Teichmann, allowed me to use material from our conversations in sermons at the University Church, which sparked off immense interest amongst the congregation, with several coming up to me and afterwards and saying, 'You know, Vicar, I think I'm rather in that category myself.'

What emerged was a widespread difficulty with the supernatural claims about God, especially the miraculous and the problem of how an omnipotent God could allow evil and suffering in the world. This was counterbalanced by a strong affirmation of the communal benefits of the life of the Church, a commitment to Christianity's moral compass, and a valuing of the aesthetics of religion – the sense of transcendence that can be felt in response to art, music and the resonant language of the Bible and Christian liturgy.

You could describe their atheism as 'soft,' in contrast to the 'hard' atheism of scientific rationalism, typified by that great high priest of the hard school, Richard Dawkins. Pullman's atheism, on the other hand, I would describe as of the soft school and if you want another high profile example there's the novelist Julian Barnes, who begins his meditation on death, '*Nothing to be Frightened of*,' with the words, 'I don't believe in God, but I miss Him.' That is exactly how so many people I know feel. The whole cultural edifice that surrounds God retains an appeal, but the central tenet is a step too far for the modern mind. The Astonomer Royal, Martin Rees, describes himself as a 'tribal' Christian, he goes to church but doesn't believe. Of course, atheist is itself a hard word, and the soft school can spill over into agnosticism, into what is sometimes referred to as 'devout scepticism,' whereas the hard school takes no prisoners and wants empirical evidence for everything.

To all of these I want to say, look, you don't have to take the supernatural and the dogma on board; you can be an 'atheist' in that sense whilst still finding meaning in the Christian story and feeling part of the Church if you want to. When you think about it, down the ages large chunks of the church have been ambivalent about the supernatural, and certainly about the dogma, if only in the sense of having a different dogma, from the Celtic and Nestorian Christians through to the Quakers. The battle between openness and inflexibility could be a definition of Church history.

My Oxford colleague, Canon Jane Shaw, made this clear in her Eric Symes Abbott Memorial Lecture in 2008 when she pointed out that there are many people involved with the Church 'who don't believe what they 'ought' to believe, but need and want to be there for a whole host of reasons, not least a desire for connectedness with other human beings. They 'belong without believing' and they are significant parts of our worshipping communities.'[1]

A similar observation is made by philosopher Charles Taylor in *A Secular Age* where he argues that as the number of people describing themselves as atheist, agnostic, or of no religion rises, so the gamut of beliefs in something beyond widens; 'in other words a wider range of people express beliefs which move outside Christian orthodoxy... more people adopt what would earlier have been untenable positions, e.g., they consider themselves Catholic while not accepting many crucial dogmas, or they combine Christianity with Buddhism, or they pray while not being certain what they believe. This is not to say that people didn't occupy positions like this in the past. Just that now it seems to be easier to be upfront about it.'[2]

In 1946 a survey of 500 semi-suburban London residents found that two thirds of the men and four fifths of women believed or 'believed more or less' in the existence of God. Only 61% of those believing in God believed in the divinity of Christ, but 25% of those not believing in God believed in the divinity of Christ. 'A 40-year-old man captured the prevailing view of religion: I think it's alright in a way, provided it's not overdone.' He captured that sense of popular indifference towards religion that has been under the surface for a long time. But would one say that he was necessarily irreligious? David Kynaston. *Austerity Britain*, Bloomsbury Publishing 2007, p 126

*

When Philip Pullman and I were preparing for our evening's discussion, I described myself as having a *secular* rather than *religious* temperament, because I wanted to dissociate myself from the Church's introspective agenda of gays and women bishops and to make him see me as a man of the world, an open thinker who looks to the concerns of the bustling metropolis rather than the reflections of the cloister. But he attacked that idea as if it were betrayal on my part, saying that, as far as he was concerned, he *did* have a religious temperament, not a secular one, implying that I ought to as well. 'What characterises a religious temperament in my mind,' he said, 'is having a sense of awe and wonder, and I have a sense of awe and wonder. It's also about asking those questions: who we are, and what are we here for, and whether there's a purpose. Some people are satisfied with one sort of answer, others want a mythological answer. Of course you can't prove that there's no possibility of God, and in that sense I suppose I ought to call myself an agnostic rather than an atheist, but I see no evidence for a God.'

The last person I interviewed, a teacher of English, Catherine Brown, made the same point: that, although she doesn't believe in a God who acts, she has 'a religious temperament' which influences the way she lives. 'I like ritual,' she says. 'Reverence and seriousness are hugely important to me - great earnestness. I want other people to be religious too. When I see a brown-clad monk walking over Magdalen Bridge, I am greatly encouraged.'

So the term 'religious' is being used to describe an approach to the huge existential questions which, in the opinion of many, a purely scientific account fails to reach. But, according to these critics, a purely theological account also fails: to understand ourselves as created by God and living in a world under the kingship of Christ is just too unscientific and too mythological for the Christian Atheist. Yet there are fertile plains between hard reason and a literalist reading of myth, much of that land cultivated by religion with insights and ideas that many sceptics just don't want to let go. Myth, metaphor, imagery, symbol, analogy, simile, jokes, are not the obvious tools of physics and scientific explanation, but they are the essential tools of being human, and, as it happens, of religious understanding. It's both the puzzle of explanation and of wholeness. If you are suffering from cancer or kidney disease in a modern hospital, you have a very reasonable expectation of being cured by science. But that in itself might not be enough: you also need hugs and reassurance and transfusions of the milk of human kindness, and sometimes additional alternative medicine, for the whole person, mind and body, to accept the process of healing.

Archbishop Rowan Williams argues that we should pause before assuming that 'instrumental reason can answer all questions about how to shape a moral and humane world and that absolute convictions about human worth are not simply generated by instrumental reason, but have a lot in common with a pre-modern view that humans stand together in a common relation, in an order which reflects the way things are in the universe.'[3] In a nutshell, in order to understand who we are, we need more than scientific explanation. Much of what we know about ourselves, from very early childhood onwards, is discovered by stories, sagas, tales of the enchanted wood, legend, folk memory, attempts to depict ourselves in drawings and painting, singing and dancing, social networking, and the daily rituals of our society. In all cultures, religion has been, and is, an important medium for translating these functions into the social fabric and it's not surprising therefore that it should hold immense significance even for people who have intellectually dismissed its metaphysical claims or become disillusioned with the corruption of its institutions. Hence the force of 'I don't believe in God but I miss him.'

So Christian Atheist is a ragged category and I apologise if I can't be pinned down by definitions.

What I want to do in subsequent chapters is to explore the hinterland between Christianity and atheism, particularly as explained to me first hand by my ten interviewees, but also in relation to my own developing theology. Given the composition of the group, it's what sociologists would call 'elite interviewing.' But these are people accessible to me who have thought about God, Christianity and belief in such a way as reflects directly on my subject. In alphabetical order they are as follows:

Oxford English tutor and writer – Catherine Brown
Psycho-therapist – Frank Camilleri
Businessman – David Gye
Venture capitalist – Nigel Hamway
Oxford undergraduate – Bella Landymore
Oxford science D.Phil student – James MacLaurin
Writer – Philip Pullman
London philosopher – Paul Snowden
Oxford philosopher – Roger Teichmann
Parent of young children – Mary Zacaroli
With shorter conversations reported from other sources

But to start with I want to describe one interview in detail, since it was the first and gives a fuller impression of what I am talking about.

Nigel Hamway Interview

Having learnt of my idea to write a book on 'Christian Atheism,' Nigel Hamway invites me round to talk about it. He's just arrived back from London and a day at Charterhouse, the private equity firm of which he's a director.

He wants to tell me the story of his journey of faith, or more precisely his journey from faith, since he has been an atheist from the age of fifteen. At King's School, Canterbury, he was prepared for confirmation by the bushy eye-browed Archbishop of Canterbury, Michael Ramsey, but jacked out at the last minute on the grounds that he didn't really believe in God after all. At school and Cambridge, being musical, he sang in the choir, attending evensong every week, until the worship of the Church of England had rubbed off on him leaving an indelible cultural mark which he now considers more an enhancement than disfiguring scar. 'It's hard,' he says, 'to have Canterbury Cathedral as your school chapel without being aware of the past strength and power of the Church.'

BM
You rejected faith in quite a public way by handing your resignation note to the Archbishop of Canterbury; shouldn't that have closed the religion chapter in your life?

Nigel
'I was admitted to Cambridge to read Natural Sciences, but changed to anthropology after a year, and consequently began to see how human groups and societies define themselves by telling a story, as in the Aboriginal Song Lines – a story that reinforces shared values. I also saw how the culture of the Christian West is shaped by the Christian story, the incarnation, and the death and resurrection of Christ and by the ethical values encapsulated in

that narrative. Of all human activity the most important is belonging to a community. OK we are tribal, and the ugly side of tribalism is that we will sometimes protect the interests of our tribe against another with fierce aggression, but on the whole belonging is good and belonging to a community is not only an inbuilt need in people, but brings a sense of well-being. Groups establish their identity by creating symbols and myths, folk tales, foundational texts. So you can see where I'm coming from: you can see how religion fits into that anthropological category. Religion is about binding people together and the glue in the mix can be a variety of agents: survival, sense of purpose, sense of mutual support, common values, acceptance of a common story or beliefs, safe social environment for the kids, music, and so on.'

BM
'But, if you don't believe in God, which would seem to be the *sine que non* of Christianity, why are you so involved with the Church and why do you give so much financial support?'

Nigel
'Social binding is the defining strength of the Church and that's why I'm there; for my family and for my community and I have some close church friends as a result, but I have other social networks. The liberal part of the Anglican church provides a number of things I value: it's a community which welcomes broadly everyone - including older, lonely or difficult people; it provides a brilliant framework for children to grow up in; in the church I go to the music is outstanding as is the musical education for the children; it provides a focal point for the community with concerts, plays, and events; my wife is an active member and I want to support her too. They even perform the music I have composed - my Easter anthem 'Christ is risen' has just had its third outing.

BM

A strange choice of text for an atheist, if I may say so.

Nigel

Yes, funny I admit. On Christmas Day I get a group of brass players together, me on the trumpet, my children and friends' children on other instruments - some of them aren't very good - but we make a joyful noise, and people leave with big smiles on their faces. The community aspect is the genius of the Church: you could go pretty well anywhere in the UK, drop in on the local branch of your church and belong.'

But there's another very important aspect of Nigel's atheism: he says, 'the moral framework of this brand of Christianity is a good one and one which I want to share.'

I object that as an atheist his ethics might be *similar* to Christian ethics, but without the authority of God and the model of the incarnate love of God, they can scarcely be claimed as truly Christian – more like utilitarian ethics, the greatest happiness for the greatest number, perhaps? Or humanist ethics – that there are natural, self-evident ways in which we must live if we want to flourish in a liberal democracy.

Nigel

'No, I think that Christian ethics, like those of every other belief system, are manmade, but I'm still content with a notion of *Christian* ethics - love your neighbour, don't always put yourself first, turn the other cheek, that sort of thing - without bothering about the need for the authority of God. Of course, I wouldn't refer to myself as a 'Christian.' It's you who have brought that into the equation with your title.'

BM

'But what are you thinking when you go to church? I ask this because I find it difficult to understand why a person would bother if there were no openness to transcendent or 'spiritual' possibility.'

Nigel
'Well, basically I say the creed – it tells the Christian story - but I don't take communion and I don't say the post communion prayers about giving thanks for being fed with the body and blood of Christ. Since I believe that the whole thing is constructed by man for man, why should I want to believe the mysteries? I've had to come to terms with the idea that we're here, we die, and then we're not here. A bit sparse you may think, especially as the resurrection is kind of central to Christianity, isn't it. What I get from services is no different from what you might get from a beautiful mountain scene. I take spiritual comfort from aesthetic experience - 'belonging to everything' – but I don't think transcendent experiences require religion to explain them.'

BM
'I'm not sure whether you fit my category of Christian Atheist at all; perhaps no one does. At first I was going to describe you as a 'sacred music atheist,' what one of the sopranos in my church choir described, when I asked her where she stood on the church-manship scale, as 'Anglo-Choral.' But I can see you could equally well be a 'community atheist' or a 'Christian morality atheist.'

Nigel offers me another glass of Puligny Montrachet and we set about expanding the nomenclature of Christian atheism. There are Prayer Book atheists (Philip Pullman and Alan Bennett), Anglican atheists (Philip Larkin), numinous building atheists (DH Lawrence?), theologian atheists, and of course all those who would prefer to be classified as agnostic, uncertain, but often devout.

Since my mind set has been formed from inside the Church, I

have always thought that you are either a believer or non-believer, you're in or you're out, rather as Jesus said, 'whoever is not with me is against me, and whoever does not gather with me scatters,'[4] but I begin to realise this exclusive categorisation is in many ways unhelpful and that what we are describing is a territory between faith and reason, between embedded religious culture and secularism, physics and metaphysics, gospel and organised religion, the temporal and the absolute, that it is proper to occupy; that in fact that is the territory where most people live.

The Appeal of Aesthetics to the Christian Atheist

'...some to church repair,
Not for the doctrine but the music there.'
Pope, *Essay on Criticism*

As I drive down to Cornwall to a god daughter's wedding in May 2008, historian David Starkey pops up on Radio 4 to explain the significance of Handel's *Messiah* in his life. Having talked of his own love for the music, picking out for special mention 'Behold the Lamb of God' and the 'Alleluia Chorus,' he describes his Kendall memory of the annual performance there as a kind of 'musical Lowry – little people going in to hear it and finding a greater sense of purpose.' Patronising? Lui? I don't think so. We are made bigger by such experiences.

In *'Untold Stories,'* Alan Bennett describes an uncannily similar scene.[5] Having mused over the transmutation of Kathleen Ferrier from Blackburn telephonist to famed contralto, and an occasion when his parents went to listen to her in Leeds' Brunswick Chapel, he writes, 'What makes music inviolable still for me, and preserves it from the poisonous flippancies of Classic FM, are scenes like that, a Methodist chapel in the slums of Leeds lit up and packed with people on a winter night in 1947 and the voice of Kathleen Ferrier drifting out across the grimy snow.'

Neither of these are intended as religious statements, but both are disclosures of the common experience in which people find some sort of transcendent depth in art, some sense of being taken beyond themselves, of being the better or the greater for having been there and heard a performance. In both cases the music's effect is heightened by context, the Bennett example eliciting both the transformation of the persons who listen and the landscape as well - even the political backdrop of post war austerity Britain.

When faced with the question whether music refers to meanings outside itself, George Steiner says starkly, 'Music means. It is brimful of meanings which will not translate into logical structures or verbal expression,' and he gives the example of Schumann, who when asked to explain a difficult étude simply sat down and played it a second time.

Forgive me for lining up my witnesses before I have set out my case, but I also wish to call Erich Maria Remarque, the writer of '*All Quiet on the Western Front*,' who tells a touching story of transcendence, as it were, viewed from the outside. The twenty year old narrator of the novel, a German soldier, is guarding an enclosure of Russian POWs - sick and dispirited men - penned in like dogs. Observing the Russians' increasing hopelessness as they stand clutching the wire fence, and witnessing their funerals as one by one they die of dysentery, the soldier is moved to compassion and questions the morality of their treatment. In a small gesture of solidarity, a kind of act of atonement, he breaks cigarettes in two and shares them through the wire, conversing with those who speak a little German. He describes 'a musician amongst them who says he used to be a violinist in Berlin. When he hears that I can play the piano, he fetches his violin and plays. The others sit down and lean their backs against the fence. He stands up and plays, sometimes he has an absent expression which violinists get when they close their eyes; or again he sways the instrument to the rhythm and smiles across to me.'

Who knows what is contained in that 'absent expression,' but the *in extremis* setting of this poignant recital evokes liberation and memory – that combination of wishful thinking and mournful recollection, which is the transcendent dream of the captive.

*

Talking to Christian atheists about their reasons for hanging on to the coat-tails of religion, nearly all say that art, music and literature provide their closest access to religious experience and the reason many of them are still involved with institutional Christianity is because of its commitment to the search for truth through beauty. Many theists of course feel exactly the same about art, finding a sense of God not only in the rich heritage of religious buildings and liturgical words and music, but in art galleries, books and concert halls. What is it, then, about art, in the broadest sense, that stimulates the experience of the transcendent, of seeing beyond, of finding as it were a new dimension?

First we should say, perhaps, what we mean by 'transcendence.' The traditional definition suggests something beyond human experience and reason, possibly divine, so that in religious writing God (the Divine) is sometimes referred to as 'the transcendent.' But the uplifting experience of art, so far as I can see, is clearly of this world and not supernatural and maybe to do with finding new layers of meaning – a point to be explored in greater detail later in this chapter.

But before discussing that I should make some reference to those who refuse to close the door on the metaphysical possibility, amongst these the famous German Catholic theologian, Hans Küng, who in 1991 published a short book, '*Mozart – Traces of Transcendence,*' in which he discusses his own sublime experience listening to Mozart's music. Just a hint, maybe, of Shaffer's play, '*Amadeus,*' in which the court composer, Salieri, fears his rival, Mozart, has a direct line to God. But the theologian is careful to be on his guard against commandeering art for religion. In a personal tribute to the music of Mozart, Küng writes: 'In this overwhelming, liberating experience of music, which brings such bliss, I can myself trace, feel and experience the presence of a deepest depth or a highest height. Pure presence, silent joy, happiness. To describe such experience and revelation of transcendence religious language still needs the word God...'[6] Karl Barth felt the same.

In defence of the intellectual integrity of thinking this way, the philosopher of religion, John Cottingham, talks about transcendence in an analogy with the *Big Bang*. Obviously we cannot prove the *Big Bang* by doing an experiment (that would mean creating the universe all over again), but we are able to deduce it scientifically from background traces of radiation in the universe. Similarly, he argues, we might say that in the experiences of transcendence found in music, art, literature and science 'one can discern in the world unmistakable traces of that unexperiencable reality that transcends it.'[7] The point of the analogy is that the *Big Bang* is not a matter blind faith, nor the result of experimental science, yet here is a theory widely respected. Similarly, with a metaphysical view of transcendence: to take it seriously is not blind faith, neither is it experimental science, yet intellectually speaking the theory might win some respect.

At the risk of being accused by more conservative colleagues of supping with the devil, I'm inclined to agree with Richard Dawkins on this one, that this might be just another version of the argument from design - that eighteenth century idea that a world of such amazing complexity must necessarily have a divine architect, as Addison's hymn puts it:

'The spacious firmament on high,
with all the blue ethereal sky,
and spangled heavens, a shining frame,
their great original proclaim.'

Dawkins asseverates: 'obviously Beethoven's late quartets are sublime. So are Shakespeare's sonnets. They are sublime if God is there and they are sublime if he isn't. They do not prove the existence of God, they prove the existence of Beethoven and Shakespeare...If there is an argument linking the existence of great art to the existence of God, it is not spelled out by its proponents.'[8]

*

Somewhere between the religious view that transcendent experience can lead to intimations of the divine, and the rational view that it is simply a heightened level of feeling, a neuromechanical matter and no more, there lies a kind of Platonism, based particularly on his idea of 'forms': that justice, goodness and beauty (for example) exist as perfect paradigms and universals in some other world, and when we speak of these things, or try to apply them in our daily lives, we experience an imperfect version or shadow of that ultimate reality.

The novelist Iris Murdoch stands at that crossroads. In her novels, as Karen Armstrong points out, her characters typically have what seem to be numinous experiences when contemplating art or nature, so much so that you might suppose this to be the experience of Murdoch herself. I knew Iris Murdoch, both in her heyday and in those last years when she suffered from Alzheimer's and was looked after so attentively by her husband, John Baillie. Sometimes I would find her in the University Church, standing in the North aisle, not praying, but seeming to contemplate a wider mystery. Armstrong believes that Murdoch had developed a form of secular mysticism, and that what her characters are portrayed as experiencing is a form of revelation, similar to what religious people describe as God or the sacred. You can imagine Armstrong, the ex-nun, wrestling with vocation and God (prior to the 'ex' factor, that is), of a sunny afternoon in the convent garden, entering Murdoch's eccentric world and deciding: 'If an unbeliever could experience the same kind of ecstasy as a Christian mystic, it seemed that transcendence was just something that human beings experienced and that there was nothing supernatural about it.'[9]

But Iris Murdoch was also an Oxford philosophy don who taught at St Anne's College and she sets out what she thought (at least in 1968) in a little known book, *The Sovereignty of Good*, three essays on Plato and the philosophy of morality, art, beauty and the self. The brackets are important since her biographer, Peter Conradi, tells us that by 1968 she was having second thoughts about her Platonist views and expressed her uncertainty in her novels of that same period *The Time of the Angels* and *A Fairly Honourable Defeat*, where one character abandons his monograph on Plato and another has his work torn up by his son. But second thoughts don't necessarily diminish an argument and what emerges for me as the main point of that splendid book is that goodness is a 'transcendent reality,' and 'virtue is the attempt to pierce the veil of selfish consciousness and join the world as it really is.' Interestingly, she links two of the main strands of Christian Atheism, the moral compass and aesthetics, and regards them as part and parcel of the same phenomenon. But she is clear that the experience is entirely physical and fears that the seductive thought that we're seeing God in such circum- stances 'is always a consoling dream projected by humans on an empty sky.' Even so, while she doesn't accept the idea of God to solve the dilemma, she does quote St Paul's advice to the Philippians - to contemplate whatever is true, honest, just, lovely and of good report - as a fine example of how to access the transcendent. But then there is a massive overlap between religion and platonic secularism, the one speaking of losing life to save it, the other of the virtue of suppressing the ego. In Murdoch's words: 'The appreciation of beauty in art or nature is not only...the easiest available spiritual exercise; it is also a completely adequate entry into...the good life, since it *is* the checking of selfishness in the interest of seeing the real.'[10]

I interpret her view as this: that there is something beyond ordinary experience; a deeper meaning than at first appears on the surface, which can be seen through unselfish attention to the good. This is what she says:

> 'The chief enemy of excellence in morality (and also in art) is personal fantasy: the tissue of self-aggrandising and consoling wishes and dreams which prevents one from seeing what there is outside one. Rilke said of Cezanne that he did not paint 'I like it,' he painted 'There it is.' This is not easy and requires in art or morals a discipline. One might say here that art is an excellent analogy of morals, or indeed that it is in this respect a case of morals. We cease to be in order to attend to the existence of something else, a natural object, a person in need. We can see in mediocre art, where perhaps it is even more clearly seen than in mediocre conduct, the intrusion of fantasy, the assertion of self, the dimming of any reflection of the real world.'[11]

*

The effect of art, literature and music is multi-layered. Writing uses metaphor, ambiguity and symbolism as well as storytelling to communicate personal ideas about what it is to be human. Music uses harmony, tunes, form, dissonance, resolution, major and minor, piano and fortissimo, the voice, strings, reeds, and the sound of the trumpet to create a multi-layered experience capable of moving us. Art employs drawing, sculpture, colour, materials, DVD installations, and plain concepts – it is often both conceptually and physically layered, the old masters themselves painting layer after layer of tempora paint to build up an image.

But what analysis can we give of the experience of transcendence? What measurements can we make? If the ineffable is not really ineffable at all, but can be reduced to neuroscience, let's have the explanation. I can feel my critics getting jumpy. I can hear them complaining this priest begins to sound like an atheist himself. But I will do my best to give an account of how I think this works, however partial and incomplete my attempt will be. For a start, no one really knows quite how music works, how it affects the brain, or how at its most sublime it moves the hearer. Steiner's claim that music is brimful of meanings, which will not translate into logical structures or verbal expression, gives a clue. Yes, there are structures such as sonata form, but they tell us no more about the music than fourteen lines and a rhyme scheme tell us about a sonnet. Often words are set to music and then the meaning is more articulate – sound can enhance a sense of height, depth, sadness, joy, fear, loss or triumph. Important too is the expression in sound alone of emotion, intensity, imagination, dream, dissonance and resolution. The German baritone, Thomas Quasthoff, asked on the radio to say what he thought people might get from the music of Haydn (which he was to perform in London that week) in these 'economically troubled times' replies, 'escape into another world of music. The deep wish of humanity is to reach the harmony which this music expresses.'

Understanding how language works is a little easier, since words are our principal tools for digging down into meaning. Yet we sometimes forget that language has to meet many different situations and circumstances to which it must adapt: scientific language describes the testable hypothesis – if you heat a liquid to a certain temperature it will turn to gas; philosophical language likes to be very precise – hence the recurrence of the phrase, 'it depends what you mean by X'; legal language means to exclude any possibility of doubt in the application of a law; religious creeds try to define beliefs and capture orthodoxy. But not all language has such a definitional purpose: poetry uses imagery, symbolism and metaphor to expand an idea, and to evoke a personal response. There is a recording of Philip Larkin reading his poem, *The Trees*:

'The trees are coming into leaf

Like something almost being said...'

As he reads the second line he pauses after 'something,' and longer after 'being,' before accentuating a quizzical, but emphatic, *said*; underlining his search for an image, so that you see the cleverness of the analogy – the emergence of spring is a kind of speech. It is a poem about the annual renewal of nature, and how spring's freshness can remind us of our mortality and growing older, a matter of ultimate concern to all of us and in a sense, therefore, religious. The third stanza develops the metaphor, referring to the trees as 'unresting castles' (castles in the air?), and what they 'say' is the surprisingly positive message, for Larkin, 'begin afresh.' This is a simple example, but an example nevertheless, of how the poet layers meaning, piling up the metaphorical strata, so that ideas interact and interplay to give the reader fresh ways of seeing, new ways of interpreting and understanding, which when it happens is immensely stimulating and transporting.

Writing in the very splendid Liverpool literary magazine *The Reader*, (Spring 2008) AS Byatt describes her delight, as an author, in making connections 'of which metaphor-making is one of the most intense' and 'perhaps the fundamental reason for art and its pleasures.' She goes on to describe an interdisciplinary project, undertaken by Professor Philip Davis of Liverpool University's English faculty and university neuroscientists, in which observations are made of the brain's response to Shakespeare's syntax. Evidence shows that when the subjects hear Shakespeare's words, especially his innovative formation of verbs from nouns, the connecting links between neurones 'light up' for longer than they do with ordinary sentences. Byatt concludes:

'Maybe...we delight in puns because the neurone connections become very excited by the double input associated with all the stored information from two arbitrarily connected things or ideas...It occurred to me that metaphors might arise from the same neuronal excitement – a double input, a strengthened connection.'[12]

When I mention this to my philosopher colleague, Anita Avramides, she says that in her study of the philosophy of mind this multi-layering seems to lie at the heart of meaning and is the basis of thought. That is to say, our ability to grasp meaning, and what it is *to be*, has more to do with metaphor and symbol than with unambiguous definition. So the biggest question of all, 'Who am I?' is illuminated by language of this kind. I can just see those metaphors and puns lighting up like glow-sticks at a children's party in a moment of disclosure that others from time to time have described as the penny dropping, the eureka moment, a blinding light, or a Damascus Road experience. These revelatory experiences will be in no way diminished when scientists can explain exactly what is going on in the brain when they happen – if anything, they will be enhanced, if only by a degree or two. The analysis will be very similar to explaining that the music of Beethoven is made by violas and clarinets – we see the musicians playing and understand the acoustics of vibrating strings, but the effect on the imagination transcends physics.

What does this mean for religious language?

I am tempted to say all religious language is metaphorical, but while that would be an exaggeration, it's a theme I find myself constantly returning to. There are of course laws and moral precepts and statements of how things are, but the bits of the Bible people keep coming back to are neither indicative nor imperative but passages that ask questions and express desire. Whether it's the parable of the Good Samaritan, the Psalmist's cry to God or Isaiah's vision for liberation and justice, there's no escaping the fact that religious language's stock in trade is a poetic imagery that expands the grasp of meaning, value, and what it is to be. Of course, it shares this quality with art and is itself an aspect of the whole artistic enterprise, not just a minor category of it. I think this is why the Christian Atheist keeps coming back to it, however reluctantly, however ambivalently, as Philip Pullman returns to the Book of Common Prayer. In a society increasingly characterised by trivia – reality TV and video games just two examples - it is probably the case that religious people, especially those who worship regularly, have more contact with poetry than any other group in society. It's what we do; and the Christian Atheist is drawn to the door like a camel sensing water in the desert. OK, a fundamentalist approach to the Bible treats a lot of religious language as if it were a form of primitive scientific text, as in a literal reading, say, of Jesus turning water into wine or the creation in Genesis; but in any more reflective approach the force of metaphor will out.

In a rant against obdurate scientism the novelist, Howard Jacobson, lets rip:

'Nothing returns one quicker to God than the sight of a scientist with no imagination, no vocabulary, no sympathy, no comprehension of metaphor, and no wit, looking soulless and forlorn amid the wonders of nature.'[13]

Rebuffing the intellectual paucity of scientific reductionism (what you cannot prove scientifically cannot be), Jacobson argues that human beings crave some other way of grasping meaning and illustrates the point in relation to Richard Dawkins' claim that the Genesis narrative of the Sacrifice of Isaac merely demonstrates the blood thirst of a god-deluded Abraham. No, rather, this is a 'hairspring parable of covenant, initiation and love, balancing obedience to God with devotion to your own flesh and blood, and explaining to a community the history and meaning of its abandonment of human sacrifice – a myth of civilisation in other words...'[14]

It needs the novelist to come up with the telling phrase and

Jacobson does the trick with 'some other way of grasping meaning.' That is what I am banging on about. Some other way of grasping who I am and what I'm here for and what I ought to do; some other way than demonstration - mystery, not necessarily divine mystery, not the mystery of lack of information, but the mystery of personal potential.

Those of you of riper years will remember CP Snow and caution: beware the Two Cultures. It is facile and dangerous to separate art and science, as if science were all dispassionate evidence and humanities all subjective feeling – a point underlined by Keith Ward when he says that a more integrated, holistic view of human knowledge is required. Maybe scientists are 'poets of the universe,' he suggests. You think of the big metaphors of science - the Big Bang, the Selfish Gene and the fact that so much mathematical modelling begins with conceptual imagery - and you see the sense of the claim.

Interviewing novelist Ian McEwan at a scientific conference for Santiago TV, my daughter asked him how he would say science has influenced his literature. McEwan replied: 'I wouldn't say it has influenced me, it's simply is part of my complete understanding of how the world works. If I want to know how photosynthesis works I wouldn't ask a priest, but once in the past we used to. That authority has now passed to rational enquiry and to me science is nothing but organised curiosity. So I am not interested in science, I am interested in the things science attempts to explain and I assume that everyone has the same interest.'

*

Another way in which we use language differently can be illustrated by these two statements:

1.   One molecule of water is made up of two atoms of

hydrogen and one atom of oxygen.
2. I love you.

If you have ever spoken those three words in earnest, you'll know they convey something quite different from statement one: they express feelings and emotions, and a sense of mystery. We think we know what water is, but do we know what love is? W H Auden wants to know the truth about love:

'Some say that love's a little boy,
And some say it's a bird,
Some say it makes the world go round,
And some say that's absurd,
And when I asked the man next-door,
Who looked as if he knew,
His wife got very cross indeed,
And said it wouldn't do.'

In the *Big Questions in Science and Religion*[15] Keith Ward teases out the question of whether truth can only be contained in the language of publicly verifiable facts. He says that some truth is like that and cites the statement that there are 46 chromosomes in the human genome as an example. That is simply the case. But when it comes to personal life, the complexities of who we are, what we think, and how we relate are not easily described, and it is usually metaphor that gives us insight. He suggests that human language cannot fully describe reality; it works for trees, people and rocks, but when it comes to trying to understand the inner nature of matter we have to use mathematics. In this he hits on the same idea that, I think, TS Eliot is describing in his poem *The Hollow Men* when he says:

'Between the idea
And the reality

Between the motion
And the act
Falls the Shadow'

Being a system of signs and symbol, language refers to something other than itself. Eliot's 'shadow' falls between the symbol and the reality, and there in that space is the potential for the creative mind to work. Not so much in the definitional case of 46 chromosomes in the human genome, but plenty, say, in the cry 'Freedom!' chanted by a group of political activists in the face of armed police. The late Oxford theologian, Maurice Wiles, drew a comparison between the symbolic force of this kind of language and the way in which historical events can take on an emblematic function far transcending their shorthand description. Take the words 'Exodus,' or 'Battle of Britain': these have come to symbolise enormous emotions of nationhood, deliverance from oppression, and survival against the odds. He also argued that the strength of those events, that have now become mythical, doesn't depend on the accuracy of the historical accounts behind them, but in the association and what they evoke. He believed religious language is also symbolic in this way and that, on the whole, it should not be treated 'on a par with ordinary, everyday, factual language.'

But the Christian Atheist will still be suspicious of the shadow between idea and reality in case I should try to slot God in, right there under her nose. And it's true, I might. That is to say, for the religiously inclined person, the experience of that hinterland between symbol and reality is a rich source for spiritual reflection. As I reach beyond the symbol to the possibilities it suggests, I am closest to the divine disclosure I seek. But I don't want the Christian Atheist to be put off for this reason, or to draw back like a scientistic atheist for fear of sentimental emotionalism or being trapped into unverifiable speculation.

Visual Art

In the 2003 BBC Reith Lectures, the Indian neuroscientist, Professor Ramachandran, tries to explain how art works, and gives a fascinating account of the function of symbolism. A well-known experiment with seagull chicks shows that when they are hatched they peck at the yellow and red beak of their mother, asking for food. If you disembody the beak, they still peck at it, and if you take a stick and paint it yellow with red stripes, the baby bird goes mad for it. The theory is that this exaggerated symbol of 'beakness' delights the chick. It lights up its neural pathways with big neon signs screaming, *food, survival*.

I find myself easily persuaded by this analysis. Isn't exactly the same thing happening when I look at Matisse's famous blue nude sequence?[16] What you see in each of those prints is about eight blue shapes depicting the female form.

Seen together they provide an exaggerated symbol of voluptuous womanhood, so compelling, so suggestively beautiful, that many people have a copy on their wall. The neural pathways light up and, for the male at least, the big neon sign says, Survival. For the female (since many females also have the picture on their wall) I imagine the picture also says, Survival, but in a different way, symbolising both fecundity and what it is to be Woman.

Well, art is not as simple as that, I know; exaggeration itself is not art. Why does Picasso stand out, why does Matisse stand out? There are other factors: manual skill, social context, the markets, what critics and art historians have to say. And, anyway, symbolist art is easier to explain in this way, you might argue, than a conventional eighteenth century landscape, although, according to Denis Dutton in *The Art Instinct*, even here there are symbols of survival. He proposes that evolution has developed in us an appreciation of landscape in art through the instinctive need of our forebears of the Pleistocene period to find, as a matter of life and death, a place where food was available, a supply of water – streams, lake – and preferably a tree that could be climbed as a means of escape.

So what? What interests me is whether the richest human experiences – love, awe, beauty, aesthetic pleasure, religion – are diminished or enhanced by scientific explanation; or whether scientific explanation simply isn't really relevant to these values at all.

In the same Reith Lectures, Professor Ramachandran makes an extraordinary statement about the brain:

'Even though it's common knowledge these days, it never ceases to amaze me that all the richness of our mental life - all our feelings, our emotions, our thoughts, our ambitions, our love life, our religious sentiments and even what each of us regards as his own intimate private self - is simply the activity of these little specks of jelly in your head, in your brain. There is nothing else.'

Nothing else? Can you really reduce all these qualities of life to neural pathways? Once again, to do so seems very like the reductionism of saying that music is only the wavelength of a vibrating violin string. That explains how it works, but not what it means; and what it means is the transcendent bit, the bit beyond. It seems to me that feelings, thoughts, love life, ambition each have a cashable reality beyond those electrical impulses in the jelly of the brain: for example, love life might lead to marriage, children and family; ambition might lead to great creative achievement, or, on a bad day, to war or cheating at the ballot box.

I don't wish to diminish the importance of brain research in any way and can see that a mechanical approach has many useful applications in medicine and psychology, such as the use of drugs to balance the chemistry of the brain in the treatment of mental illness. As a part of the body, the brain is not unlike other organs, delicate but susceptible to physical treatment. In the same way, we might think a malfunctioning brain explains certain behaviours. We might, for example, properly decide to exonerate, at least partially, a criminal action on grounds of diminished responsibility - if only we had been able to control the impulse in the jelly, the rape would not have been committed. But the impulses have ramifications beyond themselves, a reality beyond themselves, an effect on other people beyond themselves.

Wherever we're coming from - poet, physicist, priest - we're likely to be fascinated by the 'something more' of experience, since it's here we begin to find depth and significance - what I have called the transcendent. But no one can claim exclusive rights to the territory. The scientist is driven by the perceived need for empirical evidence, the theologian by the search for God, the art critic by the love of making connections, and, in the case of the Liverpool University research, at least one literary critic taking an interdisciplinary approach between science and criticism. Each approach can throw a different light on the broad theme, but no approach is entire unto itself, however much the more fundamentalist exponents would claim.

*

Mapping the brain
Are some people better at sensing transcendence than others? Professor Ramachandran finds the beginning of a physiological explanation. Apparently, the 'numbers' part of the brain is next door to the 'colour' part; and there are cases where the two run into each other causing a person to see numbers in colour; e.g. all 2s as red or all 5s as blue. In an experiment he fills a page with random 5s and 2s, but hides a triangle of 2s within in. Normal people take thirty seconds to find the triangle, but the 'synes-

thetes,' who see numbers in colour, identify it immediately because there is a triangular block of colour on the page.

One curious fact about the phenomenon of synesthesia, of which seeing numbers in colour is an aspect, is that it's much more common among artists, poets, novelists – 'flaky types' according to Ramachandran – than other people; research suggests up to seven times more common. (It would be interesting to get some statistics on how many synesthetes are also religious types.) Why should this be? Because, artists, poets and novelists are very good at metaphor, linking seemingly unrelated concepts in their brain.

The scientist must call a spade a spade, but in a poem read by many at school, called *Digging,* Irish poet Seamus Heaney describes how his father and his grandfather before him were experts at digging and how their history, and in a sense Ireland's history, could be described in the metaphor of digging. The poet is less adept with a spade, but good with a pen. The poem begins:

'Between my finger and my thumb
The squat pen rests; as snug as a gun.'

The pen nestles into his body as well as the spade nestles to his father's. The gun image suggests that the pen is mightier than the sword and that it might have been a better weapon in Ireland's sectarian history than the terrorist's gun. The closing lines of the poem are almost identical:

'Between my finger and my thumb
The squat pen rests.
I'll dig with it.'

Digging with a pen is, in a sense, absurd - far too small to dig the soil. So dig what? The brain knows how to make the connection and enjoys doing so: we can excavate history with a pen, grow new ideas with a pen, and, if a writer, do a day's work with a pen. And we understand the full force of that image despite the fact that these sentences I now write have never seen a pen, or smelled a whiff of ink, but have been typed directly into my computer memory. These connections are not unlike jokes – puns or the unexpected juxtaposition of incongruous ideas – and our laughter is a sure sign of the neural pathways lighting up. Seeing the funny side of a situation is about seeing it in another layer of meaning and getting it into a different perspective.

Conclusion

I've been exploring why some non-theists are, so to speak, fatally attracted to the aesthetic side of religion, especially the possibility of transcendence offered by aesthetic experience. I have tried to illustrate various approaches to the question:

1. That God is revealed through transcendence
2. That truth is revealed through getting outside of oneself
3. That art exposes many layers of possibility we may not previously have seen for ourselves
4. That neuroscience is beginning to explain what happens in the brain when we have such experiences

Julian Barnes sums it up well when he suggests that 'art and religion will always shadow one another through the abstract nouns they both invoke: truth, seriousness, imagination, sympathy, morality, transcendence.' They shadow one another. The dividing line between them is so blurred, there's so much overlap, it can be an unsettling zone for both Christian and Atheist. It's no accident that from time to time religion has railed against the graven image, burned books and banned plays; and no surprise that the Atheist has felt the tension between reason and emotion and been suspicious lest the feeling aroused by great art draw him or her to the hinterland of faith.

We have considered the possibility that our ability to uses metaphor, symbol and analogy might be the basis of thought and lie at the root of what it is 'to be.' We are all synesthetes and it's part of our physical nature to make mental connections and cross-references in the mind. Despite all his research, or perhaps because of it, Professor Ramachandran still thinks we are like 'angels trapped inside the bodies of beasts, craving transcendence and all the time trying to spread our wings and fly off.'

I wouldn't claim transcendence leads to the supernatural, but that the deep things we see through it are where God is to be found. God in the natural order, in other words.

The Moral Compass

Near the top of the Christian Atheist wish list comes the so called Christian 'moral compass.' As far as I am concerned, not an endearing term, suggesting no more than an approximate ethical direction, but one that crops up so much in conversation I've adopted it here. In an obvious sense it is surprising that Christian Atheists should be attracted by an ethical system that places God at the root of all morality. In the Old Testament God is the lawgiver and by the time of the late New Testament 'God is love,' the source of goodness and the moral principle behind all that is. So, if you don't believe in God Christian ethics would seem baseless and empty.

In the hard atheist critique, this observation is usually followed by cataloguing the moral inconsistencies attributed to God. According to the Bible, God approves some very questionable ethical positions: racial prejudice in his preferential treatment of the 'chosen people,' acceptance of slavery, excessive punishments such as stoning, and the repression of women, who have no rights and are the property of their fathers or husbands. Such moral inconsistencies are evident in the New Testament too: slavery, women as second class citizens, animal sacrifice and the repellent idea that Jesus' 'sacrificial' death was required to satisfy a stubborn God unable to temper justice with mercy. If you add to this the cruelties of the Church, epitomised by one terrifying word, *Inquisition*, the critic might claim game, set, and match against God. If it is true that the scriptures were dictated by God, then that criticism is fair. But if instead these texts show a society trying to justify its political ambitions and its social mores by reference to God, then it's a hollow victory and more susceptible to an anthropological analysis.

In the debate between Socrates and Euthyphro, Plato asks a key question for this discussion: is a thing good because it is loved by the gods, or do the gods love what is good? In monotheistic terms: is a thing good because it is loved by God, or does God love what is good. The conundrum has been often debated without any black and white answer emerging, some people even claiming that it poses a false dichotomy, since the gods of ancient Greece were capricious and therefore what they chose to love was not necessarily good, whereas the Christian God, understood as perfect and unchanging, is the definition of goodness. But let's not belittle the point. In a basic, traditional Christian understanding, a good and moral God is the ground of being and the source of all value. Even if you don't believe in God, you might still take the view that there are self-authenticating values evident in the natural order such as the right to life, dignity, benevolence, freedom, or the need for social order. You might note, for example, that in different societies some practise monogamy and others polygamy, but you nevertheless recognise beneath these apparently conflicting moralities a commonly perceived need to regulate and safeguard marital relationship. In contemporary societies, where many regard marriage as outmoded or unnecessary, this continues in legislation protecting the financial interests of people in established partnership. Some questioning theists also take the second view, that God embraces natural, self-evident values, although it has to be said that the notion of God does seem rather weakened by this position, but it could be argued in the long view that natural values nevertheless emanate from a creator God. A third view is that nature is value-neutral, so neither God nor nature provides a moral imperative and ethics is essentially pragmatic, about what humans prioritise and how they decide best to live together.

In my quest to understand what makes the Christian Atheist tick, Nigel was the first person I interviewed. He had obviously thought about the ethical side.

Nigel

'Of all human activity the most important is belonging to a community. OK, we are tribal and the ugly side of tribalism is that we will sometimes aggressively protect the interests of our tribe against another, but on the whole belonging is good and belonging to a community brings a sense of well-being. Groups establish their identity by creating symbols and myths, folk tales, foundational texts. So you can see how religion fits into that anthropological category. Religion is about binding people together and the glue in the mix can be a variety of agents: survival, sense of purpose, mutual support, common values, acceptance of a common story or beliefs, safe social environment for the kids, music, and so on.'

BM

'But, if you don't believe in God, why are you involved with the Church?'

Nigel

'I'm there for my family and for my community. I like the fact that broadly everyone is welcome, including older, lonely or difficult people; it provides a brilliant framework for children to grow up in. In the church I go to the music is outstanding. On Christmas Day I get a group of brass players together, me on the trumpet, my children and friends' children on other instruments - some of them aren't very good - but we make a joyful noise, and people leave with big smiles on their faces. The community aspect is the genius of the Church: you could go pretty well anywhere in the UK, drop in on the local branch of your church and belong. The moral framework of this brand of Christianity is a good one and one which I want to share.'

BM

'It seems to me that your ethics might be *similar* to Christian ethics, but without the authority of God and without the model of the incarnate love of God, they can scarcely be claimed as truly Christian. I'd call you a utilitarian or a humanist because what you're talking about are the natural, self-evident ways in which we must live if we are to flourish in a liberal democracy.'

Nigel
'No, I am committed to *Christian* ethics: love your neighbour, don't always put yourself first, turn the other cheek, that sort of thing - without bothering about the need for the authority of God. Christian ethics just like those of every other belief system are manmade.'

Next I talked to one of my philosopher friends, Roger, who moves the argument on another stage. He had begun by talking about what it was like to be a non-believer singing in the church choir, finding in the service of choral evensong an aesthetic of reflectiveness.

Roger
'Aristotle asked the question what is most worth living for and came up with the answer: the contemplation of what is. Perhaps the exercise of contemplating *what is* inevitably poses the question, how shall I *be*? One very important idea in Christianity which isn't really there in ancient Greek thought comes through in Christ's teaching on attitudes to the sick, the poor, the deformed, and the sinful. What is quite striking is how he identifies *himself* with such people, as where he tells his disciples, at the end of Matthew's Gospel, that in visiting the sick or imprisoned, they are visiting him. The grand idea in Christianity is the ethical one - Christ's teaching on attitudes to the sick, the poor, the deformed, and the sinful.'

'When genuinely felt and practised, such compassion is not only good for the sick and the poor, but also for the healthy and well-off, since it is morally edifying to think of others in this way and never to forget their condition. It expands the soul immeasurably not to despise, not to shun.'

BM
'I didn't expect to hear you use the word soul.'

Roger
'Just a metaphor...'

BM
'But what you say is surely another version of utilitarianism.'

Roger
'Such concern for others is much more than the utilitarian idea of just trying to minimise suffering; different from the instrumentality of putting more money into the NHS, or building quake-proof buildings in cities prone to earthquakes – not that there's anything wrong with that. It is to do with the moral subtlety of seeing humanity even when it is most crippled. Do you remember the simpleton girl, Lizaveta, in Dostoevsky's *The Brothers Karamazov*? She bears a child after having been raped by Fyodor Pavlovich, who subsequently claims rape matters less in this situation because she is a simpleton. I would say that rape is *even more* evil because she is a simpleton. Anyone who understands the Christian ethic would recognise this.'

Thus, not only is Roger an atheist, but the way he sees the world is in one important respect distinctively Christian; so perceptively Christian, in my view, as to constitute a brilliant insight into the nature of Christian moral teaching. Moreover, he has identified something in Christian ethics that seems to him unique and not obvious in other ethical systems. What is it?

I think what both Nigel and Roger pick up on is that, at least in the gospel tradition of Christianity, the moral vision and example of Jesus shines through, pushing metaphysics and creedal beliefs into second place. It depends to a large degree on the kind of person Jesus was; the principles at work behind his manner of living and teaching. In short, what was his character? Believers will of course answer that he was God incarnate and that explains his character, but it is also reasonable to say that he was simply a very good man, who derived his ethics from an intense sense of God. In classical Christianity this latter belief is the heresy of adoptionism, posing questions like, how could Jesus' death have redeemed humankind if he wasn't really God, but the Incarnation is not a narrow doctrine – it's about what you might call Jesus' *godwardness* and of course it is specific in terms of historical circumstance, namely that Jesus was born 2000 years ago into a Jewish family in Roman occupied Palestine. This historical context influences how we think of him: any other culture would probably not have produced the imagery of sacrifice so closely associated with understanding Jesus' death.

Mary Warnock suggests that Christianity offers useful metaphors and stories, such as original sin, evil, temptation, sin and redemption, for understanding ethics. These give shape to more loosely held moral hunches. In everyday life we work out standards of behaviour and their consequences by reference to stories. This is in part what people are doing when they gossip in the street about a particular situation, or follow the daily dilemmas of favourite soap characters, sifting through moral dilemmas and their possible consequences. This is essentially no different from the allegedly loftier pursuit of going to the theatre to see Shakespeare or to experience the cathartic effect that Aristotle found in Greek tragedy. Someone's got to tell morality tales to interpret the world in moral terms. Jesus' own story, especially the Passion, characterised by betrayal, cruelty, and the triumph of good over evil, functions in this way. Mary Warnock calls it narrative ethics. It has something in common with what philosophers call 'virtue ethics' or the ethics of character.[17] Both prioritise the narrative of moral behaviour over rules. Indeed, this ethical insight runs deep in the veins of Christian understanding, where law is transcended by grace. How shall I be? Well, think of the implications of the Good Samaritan story. It was a foreigner who bound up the wounds of the afflicted Jew. Go and do thou likewise. Typically, Jesus provides big general ethical priorities in a broad brush, paradigmatic approach. Who can be in doubt that he approaches the ethics of conflict from a pacifist base – turn the other cheek, go the extra mile, love your enemy? Or that his spirituality is radically anti-materialistic – sell all you have and give it to the poor, it's easier for a camel to get through the eye of a needle than the rich man to enter the kingdom of heaven. Or that his ethics of the self involves banishing the inner demons of ego – you must lose your life to save it, and accept that the last will be first and the first last. He's against obsessional adherence to the rules: for example, he upbraids the religious Pharisees for going to the extreme of tithing mint, dill, and cummin, while neglecting justice, mercy and faith (Matthew 3.24). He'd have a field day with local authority jobsworths, petty bureaucrats and the political correctness thought police, who stifle creativity with their repressive rule books. Nigel and Roger have tuned in to this Christian vision – not unique, but uniquely expressed in the gospels.

Narrative ethics is an expansive approach to behaviour that searches out what it is to be virtuous, rather than merely asking what is the minimum the rules require, what can be got away with? That difference is highlighted in the British Parliamentary expenses scandal, where many MPs defended their profligate and outrageous claims by saying that they were only 'working within the rules,' as if that were justification enough. They seemed to have little sense of the spirit of the law, or of prudence, or justice. Not that rules of law have no place, or that the Christian tradition does away with law. Quite the contrary in fact:

Jesus said that he came not to abolish but to fulfil the law. Yet goodness and virtue are rarely well expressed through any reductionist view of ethics.

*

Undergraduate theologian and Christian Atheist, Bella, approached this discussion from a slightly different angle. We had been talking about God without being able to find a point of mutual engagement, which prompted me to ask,

BM
'Can I put my question about God another way by asking what matters to you most?'

Bella (*thinks for a while and replies*)
'What matters is to find *what matters*. You see I'm a student wrestling with studenty things. Is my priority my academic work or something else? I'm tempted to say family and friends, but everyone says that, don't they. Actually I care much more widely than that. I've helped set up a student organisation, *Oxford Community Volunteers*, and work at a youth club in Botley. OK, it's a church-hosted organisation, but doesn't attempt in any way to proselytise the kids that go there.'

BM
'I know some undergraduates volunteer to do work like this, but many people think of Oxford students as privileged, self-centred, hedonists, with little sense of social conscience.'

Bella
'Contrary to what you might think, most of my friends have a deep sense of personal morality, which is, in a curious way, related to their concern about the current large-scale moral

panics - global warming, energy crisis, world poverty, and suicide bombing. The sheer scale of these things make us feel impotent to do much about them, but at least they remind us that there are ethical issues and encourage us to assess our own conduct. I've been driven to serve the local community because there's a gap in my life - and in me as a person - that no particular ambition fulfils. I suppose I was prompted to become a volunteer by the combination of self-questioning, idealism, and wanting to make a difference. Having done so, I get a real kick out of it.'

How does Bella add to the discussion? She makes the same point as Nigel and Roger: that service to the community and to the marginalised is a good thing, but her motivation is different from theirs. At one point she declared, 'I'm anti-religious and anti-church, but I can't dismiss it.' Her approach interests me because it illustrates how social or religious commitment starts from praxis rather than theory. Karen Armstrong says that 'a religious teaching is never simply a statement of objective fact; it is a programme for action.' And, addressing the Christian, she adds that 'If you behave like Christ you will discover the truth about him.' Bella seems to be working on meaning through action, finding herself not through academic theology, but in the practical out-working of human compassion. OK, she's plenty clever enough to learn the theology and pass her degree, but she recognises the gap between ideas and experience. If you behave compassionately you will discover the truth about compassion. This variable gearing between praxis and belief is so fundamental to religion I think the Church continues to be gravely mistaken in prioritising creeds over action. Whether theist or sceptic, this is shared ground. That's why prioritising *what matters* is fundamentally a religious function regardless of belief in God.

I wish I had a pound for every time I've quoted Francis of Assisi's charge to his friars when sending them out on a mission: 'Preach the gospel everywhere; if necessary use words,' and been asked afterwards for the reference or to scribble it down on the back of an envelope. Why does that saying strike a chord? Because in a radically edgy way it says that the heart of the Christian message is not what Christians believe, but how they live their lives.

Mary agrees. She brings her two children to church, but is personally ambivalent about what she believes, so much so that she soon has me defending a more conservative position.

Mary

'You can't prove God either way, so it doesn't matter what you believe; it's how you behave that counts.'

BM

'Do you mean you can believe anything and still be a Christian?'

Mary

'Well, it doesn't matter whether you believe Jesus rose from the dead, because the real heart of it is love; just substitute love for God. I come to this church because you're not trying to grab my soul. I can bring my jumbled thoughts and just live with them, knowing no one will try and convert me. You see, it's the *ritual* of going to church that's important for me - something to hang on to. I feel I need that especially when my life is anarchic and chaotic, and I hope that, maybe, by practising the ritual I'll find my faith growing.

I know I'm at sea, but I'm not worried about that. I rather like the image. I suppose I've found a harbour here where I can be at peace. Also, I want to give my children a Christian upbringing and I want them to share my moral compass, but it must be a liberal moral compass not a repressive one.'

BM

'I wonder how you can have a moral compass without some sort of moral imperatives, though. You've got to outline moral expectation and moral principles to have any sense of moral direction at all. In fact, your metaphors of 'being at sea' and 'moral compass' are telling ones, because on the one hand you seem to be content to be at sea and on the other you want a moral shape to things, both for yourself and your children. All my liberal instincts make me sympathetic with the conditionality of your position, but I want to move on to something more directed and reliable.'

If Mary is the most confused, she is very certain about one thing, that all you need is love. In this she has backing from the New Testament to the Beatles. But it's a claim that risks sentimentality. For me it raises two questions about the character of love, one metaphysical, the other moral, which lie at the intersection between Christian theism and atheism, and help to explain the close relation between the two. The first has to do with what atheist philosopher AC Grayling calls 'the lingering splinter in the mind... a sense of yearning for the absolute.' That is perhaps the crux of this book: the experience of living between definite states, particularly between secularism and religion; and that this in between space isn't squeezed out by the weight of Enlightenment and scientific knowledge but, as Philip Davis says, 'remains a profound sticking point or holding ground in the struggle for human meaning.'

Talking in my college room with agnostic students about God, I am made aware of the moral dimension: they aver that love is the greatest quality in existence, and if God means anything, then it must be love. This is followed by a long debate on whether love is just a function of the brain, or whether it has any reality independent of the brain – a big question in philosophy, which has to do with whether consciousness exists, or can exist, without brains - a point of great importance for philosophical theology as Keith Ward explains: 'The question of God is the question of whether conscious mind can exist without any physical body, and whether that mind could account for the origin and nature of our universe.' He says that it can.

But what is the moral character of that love? It is what Roger described as the 'grand idea of Christianity' – the love which endeavours to banish the inner demons of ego and to be self-giving towards others. This is not uniquely Christian – Islam , Hinduism, Buddhism, Sikhism, Judaism all teach the Golden Rule of do to others as you would have them do to you - but it is the all-pervading emphasis of Christianity. At church weddings, when typically the congregation is made up of atheists, sceptics, a religious great aunt, and a bunch of testosterone and oestrogen driven friends of the bride and groom, I'm frequently surprised by the seriousness of their response to the subtext of the occasion, when the self-giving commitment of marriage (for better for worse, for rich for poorer, in sickness and in health) is extended as an ideal to all relationships, both personal and inter-national, often through that favourite wedding reading, 1 Corinthians 13: 'Love is patient; love is kind; love is not envious or boastful or arrogant or rude. It does not insist on its own way.' That insight is understood within the sacrament of relationship and found admirable; recognised as self-evidently true.

On the other hand, at its most cynical, the 'selfish gene' argument maintains there's no such thing as disinterested self-giving; altruism always has a selfish motive. Assuming we succeed in cherishing our partners, we do it for our own benefit, because the durability of the relationship is vitally important to our own wellbeing. We visit the sick and take them flowers because we imagine ourselves in that position wanting friends; we institutionalise care into national life (the NHS) because it's economically important to have a healthy population, a healthy work force; and politicians know they won't be elected without promising wellbeing to the people. In war soldiers lay down their lives because it's their job. Pressed by the group survival dynamic they bravely rescue injured colleagues. This soon becomes a depressing catalogue of disillusionment with the human spirit. Where is nobility, honour, justice and grace? Are they mere illusions? Of course religion also knows the problem. Faced with death in TS Eliot's play, *Murder in the Cathedral*, Thomas a Becket examines his own motives: 'The last temptation is the greatest treason to do the right thing for the wrong reason'; for him the temptation to martyrdom is the temptation of spiritual self-glorification. As someone said, scratch an altruist and an egoist bleeds. Is any act without self interest? What about suicide bombers or kamikaze pilots? Even here the motive hovers between the promise of virgins in paradise and the fear of a slow and cruel death should they refuse their superiors.

But is it all or nothing? Plato advised the curbing of the ego in the interest of seeing the real; curbing, not a complete ego-ectomy. A human devoid of sense of self is not fully a person, so it seems that the self is a requirement of both moral and immoral action. Thus the stand-off between the religious self-giving view and the selfish gene view can be a false distinction. What is wrong with self interest, especially when moderated by duty, compassion and concern for the common good? When a medical scientist finds a successful treatment for cancer or a marine architect invents the fail safe lifeboat, he or she derives pride, pleasure and usually financial reward and no one resents it.

Iris Murdoch claims that falling in love is the only time you see the world 'without yourself as the centre of significance, with someone else startlingly at its heart.' (Although I think becoming a parent does the same trick). Yet even here the lover may only seem to be self-giving since erotic love is importantly selfish as well: one *takes* the other, with aggression part of it - and part of the excitement of it. On the other hand it may be the case that the Christian model of Christ's sacrifice *does* offer the nearest approximation to true self-emptying and that is one of the reasons why his story is attractive to so many: here is an ideal to hold up as an antidote before the spectre of acquisitiveness, consumerism and self-aggrandisement.

In 1971, sociologist, Richard Titmuss, explored the altruism/selfishness question in a famous comparative study of blood donation in Britain and the United States. He found that whereas voluntary donors in Britain were plentiful and had no ulterior motive, paid 'donors' in the US were fewer and the quality of blood poorer. Why? Because people desperate for money and wanting to sell their blood would be tempted to withhold personal information about medical conditions bearing on its healthiness. He wrote this up in his book *The Gift Relationship* and concluded that 'voluntary donation of blood represents the relationship of giving between human beings in its purest form because people give without the expectation that they will necessarily be given to in return. A system that depends on such voluntary giving effectively institutionalises altruism.'

It strikes me that his term 'gift relationship' is a good description of the community-ethics so much admired by Nigel and intuitively eyed up by the moral compassers. Nigel found it in 'sense of purpose, sense of mutual support, common values, acceptance of a common story or beliefs, safe social environment for the kids, music, and so on.' I see it in mutuality in congregations, a sense of the common good leading to: the visiting of the sick and the lonely; projects for the homeless; initiatives for social justice such as founding of OXFAM in St Mary the Virgin, Oxford in 1942; and a continuing discussion of what is right, good and just. When people say they value community, they are looking for ways not merely of taking from it, but of contributing to it by means of a gift relationship. In other words it's a method – one of the few available in contemporary Western society – of escaping from the moral isolation of individualism and finding community. You become a part of a larger whole, like belonging to a team or orchestra, unable to withdraw your contribution without ruining the whole. This sense of belonging by giving is enormously attractive and probably more familiar in poor economies, where mutuality is important to survival, than in rich economies which spawn the kind of self-satisfied isolationism symbolised most powerfully for me by the icon of electric wrought iron gates at the entrance to a suburban house.

As I lie late in bed on my day off listening to Joan Bakewell on the radio in *Desert Island Discs*, to my surprise, amongst her choices of music is Bob Dylan singing *Blowin' in the wind*:

'How many times must a man look up
Before he can see the sky?
Yes, 'n' how many ears must one man have
Before he can hear people cry?' (riff of hill-billy mouth organ blowing and sucking)

In that last line I realise that hearing people cry is at the heart of morality. Theory without experience is dangerous in all walks of life; and it's certainly true in ethics. Having the compassion to hear people's tears and to be moved by them is vital; especially in a society constantly in danger of being desensitised by the two-dimensional presentation of pain and suffering on TV and computer screen, where the sheer commonplace of it leads to what is sometimes called 'the banality of evil.'

*

I began this section by asking whether it is legitimate for Christian Atheists to lay claim to Christian Ethics when they don't believe in God. Isn't that a bit of a nerve? But then it isn't clear, either, to what degree mainstream religious Christians make moral choices specifically in relation to God. It's true some pray about a decision and determine how to act in the light of prayer, but even then it would be rare to reach a conclusion without taking into account other practical and cultural considerations, such as the law or what others advise. And in these decision-making circumstances what is meant by 'God' anyway: one who intervenes in human affairs; an eternal reality radiating a kind of Platonic ideal of right and wrong; the revealed guidance of the Bible? Actually, Christian Atheists seem to be happy with some aspects of Biblical guidance, particularly Jesus' teaching in the gospels, if not the more curious restrictions of Leviticus. They might also recognise the moral force of the Genesis creation myth as a guide to environmental ethics. However, if they were to look at how the churches have interpreted these sources they might be surprised by the bewildering number of fundamental disagreements, for example: to fight or to be pacifist in war, to oppose abortion or to allow women the right to choose, to be liberal or hard-line in relation to crime and punishment. Perhaps the moral compass isn't quite the right metaphor, implying as it does one magnetic North. Better, maybe, to think of ethics as a series of different coloured lines (like the map of the London Underground?) with occasional intersections and comings together along the way. We have reason and we have opinions demanding moral scope. So whether hailing from a theistic, atheistic, religious or secular base, moral views will often coincide and frequently complement one another as well as critique one another.

In my daughter's interview with novelist Ian McEwan at a 'Darwin' conference in Chile, she asked him whether he thought science capable of a more profound truth than literature. He replied that they are 'parallel enquiries.' 'Many of the truths that science offers us are... very hard to incorporate into everyday life, whereas the truths of literature are more to do with how we must live together – how we are selfish and kind, cooperative and stupid; clever and mad and funny.'

I was much taken with the idea of parallel enquiries because that's what seems to be happening with ethics in religion, secular humanism, and day to day decision making (and within

Christianity itself): people teasing out how to understand the world and how to act in it, taking their cue from a sense of what seems ultimately important, whether that is God, an intuitive sense of human rights, the moral narratives of literature, or a utilitarian view. It is somehow ridiculous, when moral goodwill shows her lovely face, to be pickily judgemental about the validity of its motivating forces, except perhaps to say that self-interest is the least attractive. We give a variety of names to that which drives us to be good and I am content to use the word God as a catch all, but equally happy with any other word or formula aiming to describe the same moral aspiration.

Philip Pullman said, 'We have to *live* – it's no good watching TV all the time. It's true religion gives a sense of right and wrong and draws authority from an imagined God, but I think we get morality from watching others and assessing whether we admire or despise what they do, sorting the good from the bad, and hopefully embracing the good for ourselves.'

Doctrine's permeable borders

A question arises whether there are certain things a person has got to believe if they are to be associated, however loosely, with the Christian enterprise. Not dissimilar perhaps from the discussion about what qualifies an immigrant for citizenship: does he or she need to understand the laws of cricket and be able to name the six wives of Henry VIII to count as English? How heterodox are you entitled to be? Several of my respondents had a view.

Mary
'I was brought up a Roman Catholic and experienced indoctrination as a child. Now I'm rebelling against that. So, please don't tell me what to think. Don't tell me I'm excluded if I can't rattle off the catechism.'

James
'I was brought up an Anglo-Catholic in the Australian outback, and went to an Anglican school where I became a cultural Christian. At seventeen I went to university and got involved with evangelical students because they seemed more loving and accepting than the others. However, after six months doubts began to grow, particularly over their interpretation of scripture, and I began to read scholarly accounts of how biblical texts were formed, edited and transmitted. For three years I tried to remain evangelically orthodox, but I simply wasn't convinced by their answers, so at twenty I decided to back my own judgement.'

Roger and Bella both expressed their reluctance, when attending church services, to join in the recitation of prayers and creeds that they do not believe, but out of a sense of community Roger eventually came to the conclusion that it would be churlish not

to, while Bella decided just to sing the hymns – but sympatheti-
cally nevertheless without feeling too great a sense of absurdity.
One can't help wondering how many regular Christians, who
would object strongly to being labelled atheist, say the creeds
with similar ambiguity. Besides, the creeds developed out of
theological debates in the 4th and 5th centuries and belong very
much to their cultures of origin, making it difficult for modern
people to say them without some sort of qualification. Many's the
parishioner who has said to me, 'Oh, I cross my fingers on this
clause and stand on one leg for that.'

Paul, who is a philosophy professor, gave a rather different
view, primarily, I think, because he was trying to tease out for me
what the term Christian Atheist could actually mean.

Paul
'Basically religion is carried on by people who believe in God and
faithfully preserve the traditions of the Church, but, at the same
time, there are hangers-on, who see there's something on offer
that they want, and they try to get it without full commitment.
But what is on offer? What is the point of the organisation if not
the creed and the propagation of beliefs?'

BM
'I would say religion is more about relationships and values, and
the term 'hangers-on' seems really rather harsh. The life of
churches is actually enhanced by 'hangers-on,' if you mean by
that the occasional worshippers, the social organisers, the
musicians and those who come at Christmas and Easter. I would
think that, as a matter of sociological fact, belief in God and
assent to creeds is not the principle motivating force for Christian
allegiance. When I was growing up in North London in the 1950s
and 60s, our whole family attended a church where there was
pretty well every club and leisure activity you could think of -
tennis, cricket, badminton, choir (both mixed and women only),

drama society, youth club, dances, scouts and guides, discussion groups, prayer groups, Sunday school and Sunday school outings to Clacton on Sea. Basically, to qualify for membership you had to turn up at church. I don't imagine, in that lower-middle-class congregation, where you could count the graduates on the fingers of one hand, there were many saying, 'because I believe so strongly in God I must belong to this church, and, by the way, what a happy coincidence that all these social benefits are on offer too.' Very often a person joined a group and then came to church out of loyalty. Of course, the process of attending would expose them to theological ideas and beliefs which they might subsequently embrace, but ask them to unpack the phrase 'I believe in God' and it would be like their holiday suitcase breaking open on Victoria Station and all their underwear falling onto the platform.'

Paul
'My childhood church was similar to yours and I don't doubt that in many respects you are right about the general life enhancing things on offer centred around churches, but throughout the Christian tradition some things other than surrounding activities have been central. Let me see, what are they? God, Christ, revelation? Once those things go, that's the end of it; you have a paradigm shift and move on to something completely different.'

Since Paul is so dogged about Christian definitions, I take his point much more seriously, even if it doesn't suit my case, and I recognise that I have backed myself into a corner. It is obviously true that not all the members of the church that shaped me were in it for what they could get. They understood their lives within the paradigm of the Christian story, where God is behind every-thing that is. When you think about it, most of those who go to church, including the high days and holidays brigade, do so because they're seeking meaning, a sense of self, a location in the order of things and perhaps a fresh appreciation of moral values.

Paul's charge that I'm in danger of moving the goal posts so far that Christianity becomes a completely different ball game strikes deep, but I am not arguing for the abandonment of his 'God, Christ and revelation' formula, rather for the open-handed inclusion of those who wish to be involved regardless of their questioning or struggling with those fundamentals. Furthermore, I think there's a subtle difference between Paul's insistence on being rooted in doctrinal basics on the one hand, and a backs-to-the-wall defence of some particular orthodoxy on the other, as for example, the Nigerian church's violent opposition to homosexuality (motivated as much by competition with Islam as by theology), or an American Southern Baptist defence of creationism against evolution. You notice I refer to 'some particular orthodoxy,' implying that there are many different orthodoxies competing with one another, which has been the case since the beginning of the Christian enterprise. Professor Diarmaid MacCulloch attributes the immense variety of what he writes about in his *A History of Christianity* to the fact that 'all the world faiths which have known long term success have shown a remarkable capacity to mutate... Many Christians do not like being reminded of Christianity's capacity to develop, particularly those in charge of the various religious institutions which call themselves churches, but that is the reality and it has been from the beginning.'[18] Paul's 'God, Christ and revelation' formula is intended, I think, not so much to create a static orthodoxy (goal posts) as to flag up an agenda that cannot be ignored by anyone who wishes to take the Christian religion seriously, even as a hanger on. Thus the Christian Atheist will also take seriously the discussion that this agenda sets out, whatever conclusions (if indeed conclusions are possible) she eventually reaches, otherwise why bother to be a *Christian* atheist. This means there is more of a place for hangers-on than Paul initially seems to allow. Philip Pullman, Nigel Hamway, Roger Teichmann, Bella Landymore, Mary Zacaroli and James MacLaurin, if I understand them correctly, each contemplates the formula with great seriousness.

However marginally a person may wish to be included, surely organised religion should welcome anyone who bothers to take reflection on metaphysics seriously; and many hangers-on, it seems to me, are precisely in that position.

The subtlety of the distinction I want to draw out between dogmatic theology and doctrinal rootedness is much the same as the difference between a 'rules' approach to authority and a 'spirit of the law' approach. This is illustrated in the history of doctrine.

Soon after the death of Jesus, Christianity crossed the cultural line from Judaism into the gentile world, raising the issue of whether new converts should first have to become Jews by circumcision in order to belong to the new religion of Christ. The debate about correct procedure on this matter was the subject of the Council of Jerusalem attended by Paul and Barnabas, Peter, John, Jesus' brother, James and Titus. After they had each had their say, they decided that since Christ's religion was not a branch of Judaism: gentile converts need not go under the knife.

As a result of St Paul's missionary work, Christianity spread rapidly to far flung parts of the Roman Empire – Asia, Greece, North Africa and Italy - where it grew and developed in local communities, rather like Darwin's finches in the Galapagos Islands. With limited communication between churches, different theological interpretations of Jesus' relationship to God evolved in different communities. By the fourth century some of these divergent opinions became public disagreements. But at the same time the Emperor Constantine had himself become a Christian, with epoch making results. First, he ended the persecution that had so preyed on the Christian mind and body. He founded Constantinople as the Christian capital of the empire and forced an essentially other-worldly religion to enter the fray of state politics and to adjust its ethics to the political art of the possible. But, most importantly, from the point of view of this discussion, he made the bishops of the Church come together in an ecumenical council to settle their doctrinal differences, which all sounds very hunky-dory until you realise that he wanted to use state religion as a political tool to unite a divided empire. Religious harmony is good for political unity, and if the churches disagree with each other, then they must be made to sort it out. The sinister by-product of this is that opinions diverging from the church's orthodox *right teaching* become not only heretical but disloyal to the state. The precedent set by Constantine is seen writ large twelve hundred years later in Tudor England where to deny God is tantamount to treason, where Henry VIII feels able to change the national religion for personal and political reasons and where those who demur are either beheaded or burnt at the stake. The long term result of the Church/State alliance is that Jesus' pacifist religion tends to be turned upside down, to be replaced by a religion that undergirds wealth, power and war.

Constantine called the bishops to a Council in Nicaea where the issue was the relationship between Jesus and God. Was it like that of father and son or was it on a cosmic metaphysical scale as suggested in philosophical passages of the New Testament such as John 1: 'In the beginning was the Word and the Word was with God, and the Word was God'? Arius, who was on the losing side at the Council, says that Jesus, while being godlike, is separate from and secondary to God. Whereas the view that prevailed, propagated by Eusebius of Caesarea, under the aegis of Constantine, says Jesus is of *one substance* with the Father; meaning that Christ and God are essentially one and therefore that Christ is divine. This became the orthodox view and Arianism was condemned as heresy. It also became a funda-mental assertion of the Nicene Creed, which reached its final form at the Council of Constantinople in 381, and remains the profession of faith common to nearly all Christian churches today. The relevant section, in modern English translation, reads:

'We believe in one Lord, Jesus Christ, the only Son of God, eternally begotten of the Father, God from God, Light from Light, true God from true God, begotten, not made, of one Being with the Father; through him all things were made. For us and for our salvation he came down from heaven, was incarnate from the Holy Spirit and the Virgin Mary and was made man.'

With language like this recited every week in churches, it is not surprising that people get the impression that being a Christian is about believing rather difficult, complex things - a far cry from the practical 'love thy neighbour as thyself.'

But well before Christianity had a Roman emperor calling the tune, there was a perceived need to preserve and consolidate the *tradition* that had been handed down from the Apostles, particularly in the face of the divisive threat of Gnosticism, a kind of pantheistic religion teaching salvation through knowledge of universal mysteries, which in many places was feeding on Christianity like a parasite. In order to counter this, authoritative statements of united belief were required, along with persons in authority, bishops, to ensure these beliefs were sustained in the church communities. In such circumstances the establishment of creedal statements seems eminently reasonable. This is a modern as much as an ancient problem. Any organisation needs an identifying manifesto, for people to know what it stands for. Hence the mission statements and strap lines that adorn the home page of any website worth its salt.

Problems arise, however, when a formula intended to illuminate and clarify becomes a tool of limitation and suppression. And it's a very fine line between the two. In politics voters expect to know what a party stands for and in consequence parties can be paranoid about presenting a united front. MPs have to toe the party line, or resign the whip. And in this convention individuals must keep their doubts to themselves in the cause of clarity of policy and party unity. Governments and oppositions usually feel there must be 'cabinet solidarity' at all costs and that divided opinion on policy matters will be taken as weakness. This is linked to an absurd fear that to admit being wrong is a sign of vapidity rather than strength of character. The Church has been tempted by the same strategy and for the last twenty years Church of England bishops have adopted a policy of 'cabinet solidarity,' fearing that any other approach might blow the lid off the church's simmering disunity, but also in response to a right wing, tabloid press that likes black and white teachings and is poised to jump on any 'woolly' intellectual reflection. When the Archbishop of York 'speaks out,' newspapers such as the *Daily Mail* lionise a bishop 'who knows where he stands and what he believes.'

I can see that it's completely reasonable to ask for a straightforward account of what Christians believe. Besides this is what newcomers to Christianity need to know. It's no good saying 'well, I'm afraid it's a matter of imponderable metaphysical questions.' You need a graspable starting point. But what form is that to take? There are the historic creeds, of course, and throughout the centuries various branches of the Church have written their own more elaborate manifestos such as the Church of England's *Thirty Nine Articles* of Religion and the Presbyterian *Westminster Confession*. Taking a cue perhaps from the Ten Commandments, some groups have favoured a short series of bullet points. An evangelical group in the Church of England, *Reform*, offers an eight point programme on: God, Jesus, sin, church, evangelism, repentance, revelation, and Scripture - all stuff the newcomer might want to know about. But these clauses are presented as irreducible conditions of membership. This is what must be believed. And when you look more closely there are some very narrow doctrinal definitions involved. The second clause, for example, dealing with sin and redemption, speaks of 'the substitutionary sin-bearing death' of Jesus. To a citizen of the twenty-first century this may seem a pretty odd concept. What is sin and what does it mean to bear it? Is it meant that Jesus takes away global warming? And what kind of God finds justice in the torture and death of his own son? The eighth clause speaks of the 'infallibility and supreme authority of 'God's Word written' and its clarity and sufficiency for the resolving of disputes about Christian faith and life.' However foundational the Bible is for Christianity, the claim of infallibility is a big ask for such a wide range of documents written by human beings over a period of a thousand years. And, it demonstrably does not resolve all disputes about Christian faith and life: both sides of the homosexuality debate adduce biblical verses to support their case.

One must therefore ask of doctrine whether there is ever one correct way of seeing things, or whether it is in the nature of theology that there will always be many different perspectives, each of which can throw light on divine mystery. It's similar to the experience encountered in Charles Dickens' *Hard Times*, in Mr Gradgrind's school of facts. 'You can only form the minds of reasoning animals (by which he means children) upon facts,' he says. But when to Gradgrind's delight the pupil, Bitzer, defines a horse as 'quadruped; graminivorous; forty teeth' etc, the rest of the children are still unable to picture a horse. Same problem theology.

By way of example, here is a classic case that has troubled theology for centuries: the question of what happens when the priest consecrates the bread and wine at the mass or communion service. At eighteen I was seduced away from the non-conformist, unadorned, puritan church of my childhood by the ritual of high Anglicanism. My parents were shocked. Having been weaned on non-alcoholic communion wine, administered in tiny glass goblets by lounge-suited worthies, the combination of brightly coloured vestments, genuflection, and a sanctus bell was a heady mix that sparked my aesthetic synapses into life. The idea, furthermore, that Christ was 'really present' in the bread and wine was wonderfully provocative. I had stumbled across a doctrinal issue that had been argued over at the Reformation in minute philosophical detail. If the communion bread and wine actually becomes the body and blood of Christ, why doesn't it look or taste like it? Medieval answer: because the *substance* changes, while the *accidents*, the outward physical characteristics, remain the same. Thus, looking like bread, it is in reality Christ's body. It was for the heretical denial of this doctrine that Thomas Cranmer was burnt at the stake in Oxford in 1556.

Today, even those to whom the question is important would probably agree that there can be no absolute 'right teaching' on the matter and it's certainly not a matter of life and death. But here is a ritual of the Church going back to Jesus' ministry itself, which has managed effectively to embody the relationship between the Christian community and its founder, most significantly by memorialising the man and his message. Besides, remembering at shared meals is a common human activity: the Jews remember their deliverance from captivity at their Friday night supper; Americans remember the first harvest of the Pilgrim Fathers at Thanksgiving; the Scots remember their national poet (and their scottishness) on Burns Night. In Shakespeare's *Henry V*, the king rallies his troops with the promise that their sacrifice will be ritually remembered:

'Then shall our names,
Familiar in his mouth as household words,
Harry the King, Bedford, Exeter,
Warwick and Talbot, Salisbury and Gloucester,
Be in their flowing cups freshly remembered.

This story shall the good man teach his son;
And Crispin Crispian shall ne'er go by,
From this day to the ending of the world,
But we in it shall be remembered.'

In religion, as in society, memory shapes lives.

But it's also because Christianity claims to be a 'revealed' religion - its truths established by God through scripture, through Christ, and the ongoing revelation of the Holy Spirit - that belief has naturally tended to regard doctrine as set in stone and incapable of change; if God says such and such is the case, how can there be any other interpretation?

*

I said that I wanted to draw out a distinction between a 'rules' approach to theology and a spirit of the law approach. It is clear to me that a rules and definitions culture is not the only available model for regulatory authority. The Bible is the backbone of Christian faith, and while it contains rules, such as the book of Leviticus, and various kinds of 'commandments,' from Moses to Jesus, the bulk of it is *narrative*, a story about what it is like to aspire to holiness or to seek after truth and a fulfilling life. And anyone who gets caught up in this story will naturally engage with it, in a kind of counterpoint where the voice of the story and the mind of the reader interplay and bounce off one another. I'm not thinking here of any fancy post-modern theory, just imagining that a person might respond to the parable of the Good Samaritan by wanting to 'go and do likewise,' or to Jesus' arrest and trial in the gospels, by being moved themselves to be more gracious, giving and loving. In a phrase that has stuck, the fifteenth century Thomas a Kempis called this the 'imitation of Christ.' How shall I be? How shall I shape my religious mind? In relation to the story of Christ's life.

My former colleague, Giles Fraser, returned to the pulpit of the University Church, where as a curate he had provoked many a lively debate, and preached about Lent being a time to cultivate virtue. Describing his work with soldiers on the ethics of war at the Defence Academy in Shrivenham, he said the army has a rule book as thick as your arm setting out the terms of military engagement; when it is right to fire, when not. But in the heat of conflict, there's no time to consult the rules; how you behave will depend on character, as in a phrase like, 'marines just don't do that.' That is to say there can be a moral expectation of right behaviour that transcends ethical rules and looks more to the kind of person you are.

Similarly you might say friendship (or love) is more than the sum of its parts. When a person says of a particular deed that they acted *out of friendship*, they are saying that what they did sprang from who they are, from the value they put on a particular relationship, rather than the weighing up of the rights and wrongs of a situation. An instinctive response prompted by character.

Two days later Giles developed the theme on radio's *Thought for the Day*. He had watched a performance of West Side Story by inmates in a London prison. Miserly critics had complained that prisoners ought not to have such fun. But, since this Stephen Sondheim take on *Romeo and Juliet* exposes the folly of gang warfare, might it not have an improving effect?

Besides, how do we learn to be good? Aristotle thought by acting it out. By playing goodness we understand morality better. And while home-spun philosophers of living-life-to-the-full might tell you that life is not a rehearsal, for Christians the imitation of Christ *is* a kind of rehearsal of goodness. Certainly in our human contact we build relationships by having a go at it. It's not just immediately perfect but needs a lot of work. If that is true for setting the moral compass, it might also be true for faith and belief, giving a new meaning to 'practising' a faith.

Blaise Pascal, who thought that faith is put into the heart by God himself, makes God say, 'you would not be seeking me if you had not already found me.' In a computing image, he means the faith-in-God software has been pre-installed at the factory. Personally, I don't buy into the idea of a 'faith gene' or God in the DNA, but a modern reading of Pascal might go something like this: anyone acting out, or experimenting with, God-related things – and this will include sceptics, Christian Atheists, and all whose fascination with religion cannot be quelled - has already discovered something of the god that Paul Tillich called 'the ground of our being.' Don't get me wrong; this is not a crass attempt to claim that sceptics really believe in God without knowing it. That would defeat my purpose absolutely. But it is to say that there is common ground, and a common methodology, in the process of asking religious questions whether they are approached from a sceptical or devout point of view.

On the black and white marble altar of Sidney Sussex Chapel, Cambridge, the Edwardian high churchmen who transformed the sanctuary of Oliver Cromwell's college into an Anglo-Catholic shrine, inscribed the words 'gustando vivimus deo,' by tasting we live in God, taken from the seventh-century Latin hymn, *The Lamb's high banquet we await*. In the process of trying to live a Christian life, holiness is discovered. It is by enacting the drama of the Eucharist, the play about the Last Supper, that meaning, and perhaps divinity, can be revealed. And dare one say that different levels of meaning are available, different kinds of apprehension experienced. Who is to say that the old lady, the only communicant at the early weekday mass in the dim pre-Raphaelite Lady Chapel, has a truer or a greater sense of God than the sceptic attending a performance of Bach's B minor Mass? By tasting, and by hearing, we live in God. With the Bible, particularly in its poetic and narrative bits, it's by reading that one joins others from the past in the exploration of religious possibilities and moral understanding. The Bible is not a do-it-yourself instruction manual describing how to assemble the theological flat pack. It's not a gaoler, but a liberator. And the same is true of doctrine.

That's why I think minimalist creeds like Paul Snowden's 'God, Jesus and Revelation' are good. If you start with the basic framework, you allow the individual space to build faith in their own terms. As soon as you start elaborating statements of belief into articles of religion, you create more room for disagreement and, in some contexts, persecution, through the desire to enforce the letter of the law. In a secular society, largely indifferent to the claims of religion, the irony is that, because they feel marginalised, the faithful are tempted to hang on more tightly to orthodoxy. It's a backs-to-the-wall reaction, a defence mechanism, but unfortunately, since people these days are less inclined to believe stuff and turning from traditional religious doctrines to art, music, sport, or drugs for transcendent experience, it can be counter-productive. In the attempt to preserve the purity of the Faith, fundamentalism can exclude and alienate many would-be supporters.

On a lower view, however, doctrine is no more than a guide to what people think, a statement of the consensus at any given time, or, as we have seen, what was imposed by a politically empowered Church. So, in the long view, doctrine is fluid and develops in relation both to internal theological critique and to social and intellectual change. When doctrine becomes intellectually isolated, it tends to be more conservative. We see this amongst fundamentalist groups where believing impossible things can become a badge of honour, a distinguishing mark of tribal loyalty, the defence of which can easily lead to a backs-to-the-wall bigotry or extremism. Examples of this would be: the bile poured out by some Christians against homosexuals; fiercely expressed views, particularly in parts of the USA, over abortion, or in campaigning for the inclusion of creationism on the school curriculum; the Zionist view that God gave the territory known as Israel to the Jews. It's a teasing paradox that the codification of beliefs and doctrines, aimed at clarity and standardisation, so often leads to division and disagreement.

*

The development of doctrinal authenticity has an interesting parallel in the development of the canon in literature. In an essay in *Prospect*,[19] Tom Chatfield argues that 'viewed from the pinnacles of hindsight, literary history looks like a stately procession of great texts. A snapshot taken at any particular moment, however, reveals a far messier business; one clogged with readers, writers, commercial obligations, prejudices and misconception.' To the Christian it might seem OK to say that what has come to be regarded as great literature is partly a matter of luck, but far more dangerous to suggest that the same is true for ideas about God. Besides, if truths about God are revealed, there is no question of chance about it. But, of course, they are also greatly qualified by the coincidences of history and culture. If Christianity hadn't grown out of Judaism, and if Judaism hadn't been shaped by the experience of slavery and migration, then the theology of liberation might never have been so important to Christian theology. Or if Thomas Cranmer had not been archbishop to that most despotic of all English princes, Henry VIII, then the language of the Prayer Book, and consequently English speaking liturgy, would not have addressed God as a despot into whose presence one should not presume to enter without a gracious invitation. Cranmer walked backwards in the presence of Henry and of God.

As far as doctrine is concerned, then, my case is that the borders between faith and scepticism are permeable, and that this is a strength rather than a weakness. As the Oxford theologian John Barton has said, 'the details of belief are not a matter of indifference, but nor are they a matter of supernaturally revealed information which one must assent to, or else... they are pointers to the mystery of God, not definitions to which we sign on a dotted line, and they do not include an implied threat, a penalty for non-compliance.' If that position is taken seriously then we can understand why the borders of the Church are also highly permeable. Sociologically we know this to be the case: people make and break affiliations, can be fickle, change their minds, do not come clean about what they actually think or believe, take a mix and match approach to religion, seeking out those bits which they find useful, helpful or consoling. At the Second Vatican Council the Roman Catholic Church kind of acknowledged this when it said that diversities in theological tradition are often 'complementary rather than conflicting.' How diverse are you willing to be?

Frank's story illustrates this, although it could equally well be in the section about ethics - as could the whole chunk of this chapter referring to 'virtue ethics.' Doctrine and ethics are closely linked and this story illustrates the permeable borders of the Church in a serious way.

Brought up a Catholic, from an immigrant Italian family, most days Frank arrives early for choral evensong at Magdalen College, where his son is a chorister. He's had an interest in psychology from childhood and, during his training as a psychotherapist, he says, 'God got fainter, but ethical teaching grew stronger. People I met as a psychotherapist put me in mind of how much I had suffered as a child. In fact, the story of Christ's suffering helped me to open up my own childhood feeling of unhappiness. In a sense God was being replaced by my becoming more conscious of things, growing more aware. What Christianity offers is a potent set of stories presaging maturity in humans. Basically, Christ struggles with desire and aggression, without resorting to a primitive, eye for an eye solution. The Christ story overcomes that and becomes a vehicle for a more transcendent type of experience, in which you can feel the sorrow of the world – if that doesn't sound too pompous.'

Then Frank loses me with talk of Melanie Klein and Christianity embodying the 'depressive position,' which I ask him to explain, since it sounds as if he's saying religion is depressing.

Frank

'The *depressive position* means, in a nutshell, that we come to accept the world's not an ideal place. For example, babies tend to start off life either angry or serene, but, with loving care a mother can help her child contain extreme feelings and understand that when someone lashes out you don't need to lash back. Also, we all have to accept that we're going to die, but the very acceptance can bring a life-enhancing outcome. So it is with Christianity: when Christ on the cross cries out that God has forsaken him, that is the ultimate human moment, because the difficult part to accept is that, in the end, you are forsaken and alone. But through suffering you learn how to love; you can't just learn love through the good times, you have to face the bad. We see this amazingly and miraculously when, for example, a parent in Northern Ireland forgives the murderer who has killed her kid. OK she might be repressing quite a lot, but the step has been made into positive territory, into redemption.'

Since Frank speaks of Christ, redemption, transcendent experience, and a new law to replace the *lex talionis*, I ask him why not go the whole hog and own up to belief in God? But no, Frank is adamant; this works without the need for God. Should the congregation of Magdalen College Chapel rise up and anathematise the heretic psychobabbler in their midst, or recognise that here is one searching for meaning and truth through the narrative of the Christian Passion story?

*

As we saw earlier, Karen Armstrong's take on orthodoxy emphasises action rather than belief. If she is right, then those who seriously engage with the Christian moral challenge are just as close to the Christian centre as those who emphasise belief in a metaphysical God. In fact, you could argue that time spent on abstracted thought about God and the contemplation of what constitutes right teaching, especially where it touches the unknowable, is an easy diversion from Christ's call for humility, compassion, mercy and service to others. For this reason there are those who would rather talk of 'orthopraxy' than 'orthodoxy'. That is to say what characterises a Christian is more to do with behaviour than belief. But clearly it cannot be one thing or the other; there must be an element of creed and an element of ethics.

Christian Doubt: Protesting Faith

In 2005 I took part in a public debate with my friend and colleague, Andrew Wingfield Digby, about the ideological clash between Evangelicalism and Liberalism in Christianity. Amongst the issues at stake were the nature of faith and whether the Bible is literally true. Devoutly Low Church and deeply charming, Andrew is the classic evangelical parson, whereas I'm a liberal (I hope not a woolly one) formed in that period in the nineteen sixties and seventies when liberalism was the mainstay of the Church of England. We became friends playing cricket together, a pursuit that raises few theological problems, despite the fact that 'playing with a straight bat' has provided the foundational image for many a muscular Christian sermon.

In the course of the discussion, Oxford medic, Alain Townsend, stopped us in our tracks by asking if either of us ever doubted our faith. We were both faced with the dilemma that as ordained ministers we have obligations requiring us to uphold the teachings of the Church, even if as individuals we question them, and consequently there was a long and startled pause. Andrew said he didn't have doubts, but was pushed by the questioner until he had to admit, well, that sometimes he did. On the other side, I failed to make a robust case for doubt-as-part-of-faith. Afterwards Valentine Cunningham, a literary critic and Christian, reminded me that doubt is what Derrida and deconstructionism bring to the Christian feast. 'Aporia,' he said. 'Aporia, deconstructionism: I *see* through a glass darkly.' I thought, 'am I being slow here: aporia, what is that?' The dictionary defines it from the Greek as 'doubt,' 'perplexity.' A dictionary of post-modern terms is more expansive: 'Wonder and amazement before the confusing puzzles and paradoxes of our lives and of the universe.'

Whereas the words 'wonder' and 'amazement' seem to me to

provide very positive tools for reflection, religious doubt can easily be seen as corrosive, especially the organised doubt and negativity of an anti-religious, political system like Marxism or the dismissive snigger of scientism. Philosophical doubt also can be experienced as primarily negative and therefore undermining of faith. Then there's the doubt that grows from resentment at bitter experience – illness, bereavement, disablement in war, bankruptcy, the death of a child. These are corrosive doubts, especially to religions under general cultural threat.

Curious to see if the *Oxford Companion to Christian Thought* could help, I found it dismissed doubt as 'quintessentially Victorian': top-hatted, whiskered citizens worrying about creation 'red in tooth and claw,' getting the whiff of biblical criticism in their nostrils, and hiding their doubts, for politeness' sake, under the chaise longue; what Matthew Arnold, hearing the ebbing tide of faith, describes in his reverie on *Dover Beach* as

'Its melancholy, long, withdrawing roar,
Retreating, to the breath
Of the night-wind...'

I shouldn't be surprised if Philip Pullman had this poem in mind when in *The Amber Spyglass* Mary Malone is asked by Will - Do you miss God?

'"Yes [...] what I miss most is the sense of being connected to the whole of the universe. I used to feel I was connected to God like that, and because he was there, I was connected to the whole of his creation. But if he's not there, then..." Far out on the marshes, a bird called with a long melancholy series of falling tones.'[23] This marshland landscape evokes a haunting sense of loss of the divine.

But there is a side to doubt that admits to a much more positive, creative interpretation and it is exemplified most clearly in the father of the epileptic boy who in Mark's Gospel says to

Jesus, 'Lord I believe, help thou mine unbelief.' He has asked
Jesus to heal his son and Jesus says to him, 'If thou canst believe,
all things are possible to him that believeth.' And then the reply:
'Lord I believe, help thou mine unbelief.' This is the real nature
of belief and the Bible is actually full of examples. Not only in St
Paul's, 'I *see* through a glass darkly,' but in the enigma of Jesus'
transfiguration when a puzzled and confused Peter suggests
building shelters for Jesus, Moses and Elijah, and in the
ambiguity of Christ's resurrection as told by the gospels:
unrecognised by Mary in the Garden, by disciples on the Road to
Emmaus, and by disciples fishing on Galilee. There is a need for
help in believing as made explicit in Doubting Thomas' demand
to see the mark of the nails in Christ's hands before he can assent
to the resurrection. But the prime example must be the cry of
Jesus from the cross, 'my God, my God, why hast thou forsaken
me,' echoing the Judaic spirituality of Psalm 22. Here doubt is
placed at the centre of Christian theology, at the very point in the
story where salvation is achieved in the death of Christ, acknowl-
edging the underlying experience of the silence of God and how,
in the deepest hour of need, however hard you pray, God might
not answer.

This is not new. In the Old Testament there is a strong
tradition of what you might call 'protesting faith': in Genesis
Jacob wrestles with God, refusing to let go until God blesses him;
Job, plagued with boils and financial ruin, argues the toss with
God but remains faithful. The Psalmist harangues God on
numerous occasions, questioning God's presence and
commitment to his people, as for example in Psalm 102. 13:

'For I have eaten ashes as it were bread
and mingled my drink with weeping;
Thou shalt arise, and have mercy upon Sion
for it is time that thou have mercy upon her, yea, the time is
come.'

It is time to have mercy, God; time to get your act together.

In English literature, too, there is evidence of the same doubt experience which is protesting but loyal. Philip Davis, Professor of English at Liverpool University, points out that in that great Christian evangelical book, *The Pilgrim's Progress*, when Evangelist points the Man, the potential Christian, to the way of salvation, he asks, 'Do you see yonder Wicket-gate?' Bunyan simply writes, 'The Man said, No.'[24] But it is not an angry Dawkins-like no. He knows the right answer would be yes, but reluctantly he has to be truthful and say no. Then he is given a second chance by Evangelist who asks, 'Do you see yonder shining light?' Of course a St Paul or a Billy Graham might say, 'Halleluiah, yes, I see the light,' but the Man manages a less than certain, 'I *think* I do.' However underwhelming that may feel, it is nevertheless a form of belief and perhaps the very essence of belief. It is positive and has the same ring as help thou mine unbelief. Davis cites other examples, including an agonised George Herbert who says to God, 'Let me not love thee, if I love thee not,' and the mighty Luther who declares, 'Here I stand. I can do no other. God help me.'

As Val Cunningham says in his book *The Reading Gaol*, 'Silence, puzzle, aporia, absence, blankness, stuttering, are as much part of Biblical theology... as their opposites.'[25] And, of course, they are, because the Bible is the writing of human beings who have, in various different ways, experienced what they identify as the divine reality and tried to make sense of it, sometimes resulting in confident proclamation but as often in awed puzzlement. This common human intellectual response should not be seen as corrosive doubt eating away at faith like rust, but as a loyal opposition to the Lord, a protesting faith which builds from within through the process of weighing experience. There's a Zen adage: 'Great doubt, great enlightenment. Little doubt, little enlightenment. No doubt, no enlightenment.' Doubt reinvigorates the question that keeps the mystery alive.

When I spoke to graduate student, James, I found a person seeking faith, but puzzled by the ambiguities it throws up.

James:

'I don't feel certain about any of my beliefs. I entertain the possibility that God's not there. But overall I'm positive. It's rather like my attitude to cancer research; I have a hunch that cancer can be beaten and I have a will and motivation to get there. Same with God, I have a hunch that God is there and I have a will to find him.'

'It's quite conceivable to me that Jesus was a mere mortal, yet I think there's some substance to the argument that he rose from the dead... I have a tentative belief, which doesn't come entirely naturally. I have to work at it.'

James' position between the wish for certainty and intellectual questioning is the natural place to be. The absolute faith position I was brought up with, and which seems to be the desired default position of the Church as an institution both historically and in the present, is exceptional; while the norm is curiosity, openness, doubt, and loyal opposition. How else would human progress ever have been achieved?

*

The conservative Christian will very likely regard doubt as *woolly* and disparage it, portraying it as shallow, lacking in confidence, neurotic, and weak. The sort of spinelessness best treated with a good dose of faith-bravado, such as affirming myths to be literally true. As Jesus said, with faith you can move mountains. Just stand up there and declare unequivocally your belief in the virgin birth, even though you know that the biblical idea depends on a misreading of Isaiah 7.14. That will show the doubters. And sometimes, just for a moment, the sheer audacity of faith-bravado induces a shock response. It seems so wild, so counter cultural, so confident, it must be true. But if you make acceptance of an impossible claim at face value the benchmark of belief, then all second thoughts, all deeper questions, all doubts, become dangerous antibodies attacking the autoimmune system of faith and they must be suppressed at all costs, however disagreeable the treatment. In Protestant fundamentalism this means exclusion from the group, but in more political circumstances (Islamic fundamentalist states) it can lead to torture and execution.

*

Somewhere between Victorian doubt and twenty-first-century fundamentalism there's a new, much more difficult question about the nature of the physical universe itself, stemming from quantum physics. The science of quantum suggests that beneath the assured cause and effect of Newtonian physics lies a micro, subatomic set of relationships that is at root unpredictable, epitomised by Heisenberg's uncertainty principle in quantum mechanics: tricky stuff explored by Keith Ward in his *Big Questions in Science and Religion*,[26] but indicating the basic ambiguity of things. Quantum theory says that the same cause can have different effects. In a significant way, then, it has superseded the idea of a mechanical universe in which everything is ordered and fixed as a basis for reality, by introducing a picture of life and reality in a state of flux. Quoting John Polkinghorne, Ward writes, 'There may be an "intrinsic fuzziness" or "ontological openness" in nature that allows the operation of further, largely unknown, causal principles.' In other words things are much more complicated and ambiguous than they seem.

But this is not to say the pillars of belief have been knocked down, plunging the enlightenment order into chaos. We still get up in the morning and go to bed at night; we set out on the road to London (or wherever) in the expectation of getting there. For Christianity its religious narrative still gives shape to faith. Just that we are learning the need for even greater openness to other possibility. In religion this must mean openness to the insights of radical challenges such as the Christian Atheist one.

None of this should be a surprise. Art, music, personality, relationship, all find revelation through ambiguity as I have suggested in the chapter on aesthetics. A student told me how he found it difficult to worship in a plain hall with curtained proscenium arch (too much like school) and much preferred the numinous atmosphere of an old and complex building. It's an experience many will share. But what creates the numinous is the combination of ancientness, half seen corners and dark spaces, which symbolise the partial nature of spiritual under-standing and the hope that more will be revealed. In music meaning is created by the tension between dissonance and harmony, between unresolved sound and resolution.

Pictorial art similarly triumphs in ambiguity. The good portrait is not an exact image of the subject, but an interpre-tation, showing something about the subject which we had never seen for ourselves, or capturing an aspect of personality that we immediately recognise, but in a new way. Whether in Lucien Freud's portraits, Van Gogh's 'Church at Auvers' or Tracey Emin's bed, truth is seen as puzzling and provocative, and through a glass darkly; yet we are enlightened by the exercise.

I am also intrigued by that other art-world paradox: the case of the great artist who turns out to be a bit of a shit; and the question that subsequently arises whether their art is necessarily tainted by depravity and should be marginalised on those grounds. Should an artist's work be banned, or snubbed, on the grounds of notorious public immorality? In terms of the doubt/faith discussion, I see a parallel in the way that for

Christianity Doubting Thomas's halo is tarnished by hesitation and epistemological feebleness in the face of glory? Yet art generally seems to transcend the unethical, which might seem odd in view of the claim that art, truth and beauty are interconnected. But there are many examples. George Eliot promotes marriage, but 'lives in sin.' Dickens is utterly moralising and fulminates against all kinds of social abuse, yet deserts his wife to shack up with a mistress. Tolstoy is intensely Christian, but terrible at his relationship with his wife. TS Eliot is anti-Semitic, but we read his poetry and find religious and moral insight there. Coleridge is a drug addict, Picasso a serial adulterer, while Mozart writes sublime music, but, as we know from his letters, is obsessed with bottoms. Embroiled in the risqué lives of the Pre-Raphaelites painters, Lizzie Siddal, their copper haired muse, gazes seductively out from many church stained-glass windows.

There's a reverse spin to this, however. Many works of art take corruption and evil as their subject, while in themselves being recognised as intensely moral – *Anna Karenina* and *Madame Bovary* spring to mind. As do, in a much less obvious way, Walter Sickert's paintings on the theme of prostitution and murder in London's Camden Town. The truth teller must be free to explore depravity just as much as goodness and honour, because the artist is digging down into the puzzling complexity of life, not skimming over the surface. Is this why Puritanism was (and is) so suspicious of art, because it finds beauty in corruption? Even when fallen, Satan remains beautiful and dangerously seductive, having the best tunes. Puritanism would protect us from distracting ambiguity and uncertainty. Howard Jacobson warns that 'it is not religion that is the root of all evil, it is certainty. And the secular can do certainty every bit as well as the religious.'

Am I wrong therefore to find faith provisional and to think it actually positive to give voice to doubt? Is it silly to assume that a religious position can be strengthened by being exposed not only to the assurances of fellow believers but also to the sceptic's questions? Some of the best theological conversations I have heard recently have been between Christians and sympathetic sceptics, such as Philip Pullman, who is not only theologically very literate, but able to encourage mutual respect of opinions.

Many church insiders would disagree claiming that anything other than an unequivocal proclamation of faith is a potential PR disaster. Not the way to win souls for Christ. I partly accept the force of that argument. You must begin with the positive, rudimentary claims of religion. But once the groundwork is in place such questioning, such *aporia*, is an authentic part of religious experience and I want it respected as much as more conservative types want their ten point creeds and personal religious experiences taken seriously. Am I foolish to suppose that the paradoxes and ambiguities related by art and the 'intrinsic fuzziness' revealed by modern physics back me up? You see, I think most of the questions the Christian Atheist is flagging up, from which so many Christians want to run, are questions about the fundamental paradox and incongruity of things, a complexity that is also the nature of faith and religion. There's a kind of theological quantum too: that metaphysics is not as predictable as theologians would like. Keith Ward has taken the unpredictability of cause and effect from quantum theory and used it to support the possibility of miracles: if there are unpredictable physical effects from the same cause, then the resurrection is a possibility. It may not fit our everyday expectations but it can't be ruled out. For me the argument works the other way about: by illustrating the unpredictability of things – the ontological openness – I am all the more persuaded of the pointlessness of muddling contemporary religious discourse with pre-scientific world views and all the more persuaded of the importance of taking Christian Atheists seriously. Not that they've got it right, but that they've got important insights to share.

Here are some practical examples of what I mean – the first a good take, it seems to me, on the paradox of faith. In the second world war of a group of Jewish prisoners, starved and awaiting the gas chamber in a Polish concentration camp, put 'God on Trial.' This was the title of a BBC2 play by Frank Cottrell Boyce.[27] The charge is that, through murder and collaboration, God has broken his covenant with his chosen people, the Jews. If he favours the evil Nazis and deserts his own people, how can he exist? In the play, there are arguments for prosecution and defence, ranging from 'God is testing us' to 'God has given us freewill,' and the claim that 'God never was *good* in the first place.' In the end the chief justice tells them, 'They've taken everything. Don't let them take your God. Even if he doesn't exist, keep him.'

In letters from his prison cell, another victim of the Nazi regime, Lutheran Pastor Dietrich Bonhoeffer (hanged at Flossenbürg in 1945 for plotting against Hitler) questioned the meaning of God and Christ for the contemporary world. Acutely aware of the Church's failure to oppose the Nazi persecution, he saw Christianity as trapped in religious institutionalism and defined by elitist metaphysical beliefs. He therefore coined the phrase 'religionless Christianity,' which subsequently became a rallying cry for some of the theologians of the 1960's who were trying to move the Church on through the paradigm shift of that 'swinging' decade of sexual revolution, class breakdown, motorways, moon landings, the *Lady Chatterley* trial and the Beatles' first LP.

He didn't mean that God was dead, but that God must be understood in different terms. Hitherto, it seemed to him, God had been located in a distant metaphysical world, in the shrinking area of unsolved problems as yet unexplained by science, and in the shrouded recesses of mysticism. People say that God can only be known in Jesus Christ, but who is Christ for us today, asks Bonhoeffer. The hereafter isn't such a big deal anymore and people take responsibility for themselves. The culmination of a Christian life has to be more than afternoon tea with aunty up on cloud nine. The old God has been losing ground. Bonhoeffer is far too rooted in traditional Christian faith to deny God, but he does say that 'God lets himself be pushed out of the world onto the cross.'

At one level this is a conventional theological view, based on the idea of *kenosis*, a word used by St Paul in another letter from prison, to the Philippians, meaning 'emptying.' Of Christ he writes: 'though he was in the form of God, he did not regard equality with God as something to be exploited, but emptied himself...and being found in human form, he humbled himself and became obedient to the point of death, even death on a cross.'[28] Some 19th century Lutheran theologians had thought that Christ abandoned his godly characteristics – omnipotence, omniscience and cosmic sovereignty – to become man. Although a more orthodox view is that God emptied himself only in the sense that he accepted the union of his divine nature with that of humanity. Hair splitting? Maybe. I am tempted to think that the 'self-emptying' of God was as far as Bonhoeffer dare go in owning up to his loss of faith in the metaphysical God. What he embraces instead is the 'Man for Others.' Not such a bad decision. Besides this is the same point made by many of my interviewees. When he says that God is pushed out of the world onto the cross, Bonhoeffer is prioritising doing over believing, action over metaphysical speculation, saying that the 'Man for Others' calls us to share his own suffering and be caught up in his own existence for others, which is a self-authenticating thing, not motivated by the promise of eternal bliss.

Given my established position in the Church, my campaign for honest openness to doubt has seemed to some insiders like treachery, usually drawing an unforgiving response and frequently lampooned. Once, when the Oxford theological colleges had assembled for their annual service, the Bible had not been put out on the lectern – 'Oh, they don't believe in the Bible here,' they said. Others mock: the trouble with you is it's all questions and no answers. Still others that I propagate a doctrine of the 'real absence' rather than the 'real presence.' But the power of many a joke is incongruity: the bishop who kicks a hole in a stained-glass window, the mad psychiatrist, the pregnant rabbi, the absent-minded professor. There is an incongruity at the heart of mainstream Christianity, the paradox that God is said to be knowable in Jesus Christ and yet is so obviously unknowable.

In his poem, *The Absence*, the Welsh priest/poet, RS Thomas is totally frank. Speaking of God he writes:

'It is this great absence
that is like a presence, that compels
me to address it without hope
of a reply'

and after discussing his failure to find any enlightenment either from ancient religious language or modern science, he concludes

'what resource have I
other than the emptiness without him of my whole being'

I don't wish to ennoble this angst or say to the Christian Atheist this is the answer; indeed she will probably dismiss it as a childish self-deception. All I wish to do is point out that the paradox of the hiddenness of God, sometimes referred to in the Latin as *Deus absconditus*, has not escaped the conventional believer.

In the most passionate passage in *The Good Jesus and the Scoundrel Christ* Philip Pullman vituperates against such double-tongued talk. In the Garden of Gethsemane, his Jesus figure says to God, 'You say nothing'... 'I can imagine some philosophical smartarse of a priest in years to come pulling the wool over his poor followers' eyes: "God's great absence is, of course, the very sign of his presence", or some such drivel.'[29] That seems fair comment. Although what RS Thomas is getting at, I think, is similar to the chief justice's judgement - 'they've taken everything. Don't let them take your God. Even if he doesn't exist, keep him'; the thought that despite the intellectual problems surrounding the idea of God and despite all the doubts on the road to faith, all that the word 'God' stands for has the capacity to give shape and purpose to a life that otherwise seems empty.

So I've got two aspects of the same phenomenon here, almost two sides to the same coin:

1. on the one side our now familiar friend whose sense of the rational makes belief in God impossible, but who nevertheless values aspects of religion
2. and on the other an insight into the nature of religious belief itself – that classically belief incorporates doubt into itself, as a kind of ongoing dialogue, a natural tension between the hope of glory and the harder realities of human experience. Although, this potentially divisive civil war between doubt and belief is bound together by faith's capacity for perseverance and adaptation: Jesus and the early Church expected the imminent end of history; it didn't come and the Church adapted. Faith has been challenged by Galileo and Darwin and Einstein, but not defeated. It can withstand rigorous questioning because questioning is actually intrinsic to the phenomenon, even if creationists, Bible bashers, and creed makers try to suggest otherwise. That's why I conclude that doubt is positive not corrosive; in the right hands, a loyal opposition and an honourable protest against God.

Rationalism Versus Religious Conviction

It's the Chief Rabbi's turn to give his Thought in the Radio 4 God slot. He tells a story of two politicians whose speeches get muddled up on the autocue, with amusing results. This becomes a parable for the vicissitudes of life, which leads him to ponder what 'God might be saying' through such experiences. He has never struck me as a naive man, but this language seems absurd. By 'what is God saying,' I think he means are there any lessons to be learnt from reflection on those occasions when your expected world is suddenly thrown into confusion. To express this commonplace in terms of what God might be saying to us seems charming and old-fashioned. Is God really using the autocue muddle to get a message across? And, if so, would that be any different from using a multiple pile-up on the motorway for the same purpose?

Stephen Pinker says that traditionally belief in God was attractive because it promised to 'explain the deepest puzzles about origins. Where did the world come from? What is the basis of life? How can the mind arise from the body? Why should anyone be moral?' Then he concludes that the more we learn about the world in which we live, the less reason there is to believe in God.[30]

Well, just make sure we're talking about the same God! No one comes to this debate without bias, without their personal axe to grind. Either you're disposed for or against belief in God, and if you say it's simply not an issue for you, then by default that's a vote 'against.' The problem in so many of these arguments is that one opponent defines and knocks down (or defends) a god that the other cannot recognise. Pinker knocks down a 'god of the gaps,' a god that provides an explanation for what is not understood; and as human knowledge increases, inevitably that god diminishes. On the other hand I suppose Pinker might dismiss my preferred interpretation of a god of virtue, love and hope as no more than bigging-up a set of admirable human qualities, replacing a lost god of explanation with a god of moral aspiration. This is the trouble with reason in relation to religion: reason almost necessarily promotes the glass-half-empty approach to God because its inherent methodology is to cut out anything superfluous and to resist expansion. The alternative emotional and intuitive approach is not only holistic and inclusive, but also recognises the irrational at the heart of what it is to be human. We are, besides, people who dream, have nightmares, repress sexual fantasies, and delight in dark fantastical imagery both as children and as adults. These are aspects of mind that, were they all to be exposed, ironed out and put in order, might just turn us into automatons. To the rationalist one has to say that it may be the case that Reason doesn't answer all the questions about how to shape a moral and humane world, but that there are other resources.

Nevertheless, rational objection to religious belief is key to the Christian Atheist. The general consensus of those I interviewed could be summed up as: Christianity - good, God - a bit iffy. David is the most decisive on this point, his story an example of someone who has given up on Christianity, but can't quite let go.

David:
'My wife was a stalwart member of an Anglican evangelical church and I used to feel awkward about not being involved in the church community with her. But the truth is, soon after leaving school, where I was a member of the Christian Union, I quickly developed into a scientific rationalist; and while I accept that the paradigm of scientific rationalism is an incomplete framework for looking at life, because it doesn't purport to address the numinous or the moral, I nevertheless take it as a foundational position.

'At the local church I found myself surrounded by highly

intelligent and successful people who seemed to believe a load of palpable nonsense. You had to sign up to circumstantial beliefs that ran entirely opposite to what I could see with my own eyes. So I joined a course, specifically designed for men on the edge of the church community like me, to see how the religion being canvassed would be explained, in the hope that I might discover there was more to it than I'd thought. I stayed the course, but remained unconvinced. I just wasn't able to believe in ideas and events entirely contrary to everyday experience.

'I think the case was sealed for me when, on a later occasion, a visiting Cambridge University scientist spoke about 'science and faith,' maintaining that the New Testament miracles happened precisely as described, and that when, for example, Jesus walked on the water, God simply suspended the laws of gravity for the duration of the miracle. But I'm still keen to pursue the enquiry and I'm actively involved in discussing these matters with friends, in a group we have started, called *The Gamma Group*.'

With all the Christian Atheist positions I've encountered, there's a problem with the irrational, with not being able to believe 'impossible' things. And in this, reason is appealed to as the decisive factor. They will say it's not just that walking on water or life after death that runs in the face of experience and scientific evidence, but God, in the common sense view of a metaphysical being, also seems unlikely. They are not necessarily antagonistic to the system that upholds metaphysical belief, or antagonistic to its adherents; simply that they can't accept that particular worldview themselves.

Nigel:
'I've been an atheist since the age of fifteen when, at King's School Canterbury, I jacked out of the Archbishop of Canterbury's confirmation class, realising that I didn't really

believe in God after all. I suspect that those who say they do believe in God have all defined their own personal gods to meet their inner requirements, and that's fine by me.'

There are many ways in which I share David's view, particularly in relation to naive literalism. Take, for example, Luke's story of the stilling of the storm. Jesus and his disciples are caught in a small boat in a squall on Lake Galilee and in danger of being inundated. When the disciples call upon Jesus, he commands the winds and waves to cease, which they do, and all are saved. This prompts the question, who is this that the winds and the waves obey him; with the implied answer: God, who has power over nature. But how are we to read this story today? If God exercises power over nature in this way, why not restrict earthquakes to places where people won't get killed? Or make mud slides and avalanches happen when there's no one about? I see God as the creative mind behind all that is, but not one to interfere with the finely-tuned conditions on this planet which alone make life possible in the first place.

But I know there is a tradition in which 'blind faith' is considered a virtue and I've alluded to it already. My eminent, and recently beatified, predecessor John Henry Newman (who accepted the theory of evolution, was interested in scientific advance, and one of the early train-spotting railway anoraks) shows a surprising acceptance of divine intervention in relation to the Holy House at Loreto. Loreto is a shrine in Italy, on the Adriatic coast, and the claim is that Jesus' family home from Nazareth was flown over to Italy by angels in three hops and landed there. Newman writes: 'I went to Loreto with a simple faith, believing what I still more believed when I saw it. I have no doubt now. If you ask me why I believe, it is because everyone believes it at Rome; cautious as they are and sceptical about some other things. I have no antecedent difficulty in the matter. He who floated the ark on the surges of the world wide sea ... who said that faith might move mountains... could do this wonder also.'[31]

A contemporary parallel was provided for me in the following story told me by an undergraduate:

Jack:
'Last term, in Turl Street, an evangelical pastor was offering to heal people by laying hands on them. While I was watching, a woman sat by the healer and, when he laid his hands on her, she fainted. It was only for a short time, but when she came round she began to cry out uncontrollably. My own response was very emotional and I needed to talk about it, so I spoke to a member of the Christian Church, but she tried to convert me. That kind of militancy gets Christianity a bad name. One of my friends had the opposite response: she was disgusted and thought the healer a charlatan, taking advantage of another's gullibility and weakness.'

These three stories (stilling the storm, the Holy House, and the Turl Street healing) raise for me the question of the nature of believing – which is a far more complex than initially meets the eye. The nature of believing is to do with how we view reality and there are different approaches. To be sure, the most prevalent view today is influenced by science.

Science attempts to describe a world of publicly verifiable facts. This forms a paradigm for looking at the world. Prove it! Prove it! This is David's take and to some degree mine. But many of the frontiers of science are characterised by provisional theories that make sense, but are nevertheless not publicly verifiable e.g. the Big Bang, the expanding universe or dark matter. Scientist Paul Davies says, 'Our measurements point to a universe filled with a kind of matter we've never seen, propelled by a force that we don't understand.'

On reading the previous paragraph, David offered the following qualification:

David:

'When religion crosses over from the mysterious, spiritual and moral into the world of verifiable facts (for example miracles, perhaps notably the resurrection), it has to square itself with science – or to reject science altogether. If it is not ready to take a bold rejectionist line, and mostly it isn't, a fair question is - go on then, prove it! My problem with the Cambridge physicist was that he wanted it both ways and I thought that dishonest (and funny).'

Then there's history. History is an evidence based discipline, but you cannot re-run the events of history as an experiment; therefore it's a matter of interpretation and there are competing perspectives. Most famously, the adage that history is written from the perspective of the winners rather the losers.

Or there's literature. Metaphor and imagery are used to evoke what it feels like to live in the world as the writer does and to see the world as the writer sees it. This is the world of empathic feeling, words, ambiguities and reflection. But it's just as much a part of reality as prove-it science.

And there's religion. To believe in God is to believe in the objectivity of value and purpose. There is no evidence for this, but in the last three millennia, from Plato onwards, many have intuited this to be the case and that intuition makes a life of faith possible. But there's a fine line between these different takes on reality. When we categorise them as I have just done, they seem to run in parallel as independent strands, but in reality they are interlocking. And many of us will find ourselves wanting to take something from each different strand. Perhaps fundamentalism in science, as in religion, is caused by the difficulty of allowing those lines to cross one another. Too muddling! Mary Midgely says that 'what is now seen as a universal cold war between science and religion is...really a more local clash between a particular scientistic worldview, much favoured recently in the West, and most other people's worldviews at most other times.'

Similarly religious people can all too easily allow their 'life of faith' to run away with them, uncorrected by the insights of empirical science; hence street healing and Newman's Loreto.

These various takes on evidence, reality and belief need not be mutually exclusive. Because there remains a question about what grounds should properly be used to justify faith. To what degree is it reason, and to what degree a sort of logic-defying inner conviction? Is religious conviction really a matter of temperament - that some people just want to believe despite what their intellect is telling them, despite the evidence? They want to believe and are ready to strike a compromise between different ways of looking at the world. Midgely again: 'Belief – or disbelief – in God is not a scientific opinion, a judgment about physical facts in the world. It is an element in something larger and more puzzling – our wider worldview, the set of background assumptions by which we make sense of our world as a whole.'[32]

In its literary context, St Luke's question about Jesus, who is this that the winds and waves obey him, seems to me to invite a broad response of trust rather than a scientific opinion. Such inner conviction is the disposition to see the positive in religion rather than the negative. It is like having faith in a person, say, an errant child or a student all at sea with her studies. I believe you have it in you to succeed, you want to affirm. Or I have an inner conviction that you have the strength of character to come good. It is itself a metaphor of salvation. I think much of the so-called 'miraculous,' inside and outside the Bible, is not a call to believe the impossible, but rather to respond to the objectivity of value and purpose, through inner conviction. In that sense sane religion doesn't ask people to believe impossible things, but to be open to a kind of imaginative religious thinking outside the box. It's only when religion is backed into a corner by scientific rationalism, and doesn't have the presence of mind, or the education, to recognise its own stories and myths in the light of metaphor that it retreats into absurdity. Besides, does the scientific rationalist never read the stories of the Arabian Nights, or tell the tales of Red Riding Hood or Jack and the Beanstalk to her children? And does she not there find some truth about human nature and our place in the world? And isn't that exactly why she reads them, to reveal something new about meaning? Imaginative stories, easily disproved by scientific verification, (who has grown runner beans big enough to house a giant?) are capable of unlocking truth.

However, sometimes people can't cross these boundaries and insist on holding two different paradigmatic views of reality in parallel, without allowing any interflow. I'm thinking, for example, of the highly intelligent evangelical scientist who belongs to a Christian fellowship that meets in the lab at lunchtime. She's familiar with philosophical arguments for and against God and also with the critical analysis of Bible texts; she knows that the methodology of such theology is similar to the methodology of her scientific work, but she simply doesn't want to approach her faith and religion in that way. She'll take the Bible at face value, thank you very much. When challenged with this clash of intellectual paradigms she freely admits there's an inconsistency, but is quite happy to process her religious faith and her scientific research with different parts of her brain, as if she has separate software packages to deal with the two aspects of her life. Presumably, the Cambridge scientist who tipped the balance for David was such a person.

In a loosely related way, in defending themselves from what they see as gullible religion, Christian Atheists are perhaps tempted to side with scientific rationalism over literary observation and imagination as a natural defence mechanism against what you might call the 'looney science' of fig trees destroyed by a curse or taxes paid from a coin extracted from a fish's mouth.

But the distinction, as I say, between science and literary imagination cannot be black and white. Whereas Midgely argues that belief or disbelief is not a judgement about physical facts in the world, Keith Ward seeks to establish Christian belief as entirely rational in scientific terms. He writes, 'the existence of a cosmic consciousness is a coherent and plausible hypothesis for understanding the nature of physical reality...there is a growing scientific world-view of the universe as holistic, open and emergent, and as grounded in a supra-temporal, beautiful, intelligent reality which may be in some sense conscious and value-oriented.'[33] This is a view which makes a lot of sense to me: that God created the universe in order that the values of God, described by St Paul as the fruits of the Spirit: love, joy, peace, patience, kindness, generosity, faithfulness, could be realised in the physical terms that we know them. Even so, having said that Christianity is a reasonable religion, and certainly not irrational, its reasonableness does not prove to be the strongest case of those who proclaim it. It is rarely the argument of reason that draws a person into faith or believing, but the exemplification of values in others, in individuals, communities, or the story of Jesus himself that causes the penny to drop and the 'leap of faith' to occur.

Loose Ends

Various takes on Christian atheism

In all my thinking about this odd paradox of Christian Atheism I have often come full circle and sometimes wondered if it's simply not a useful category at all. If the spectrum is made up of hangers-on, as Paul suggests, then David is hanging on by his fingertips and about to fall off, while Mary and James are main stream Christians just suffering from a bit of epistemological angst. The range is immense, but every time I mention the topic in conversation, people are intensely curious and want to talk more.

Of those I interviewed, Paul was most anxious to help me define what I mean by the term and, as we have seen, a great help in clarifying what he regards as the indispensable creedal basics – God, Christ and Revelation. In addition he offered these other possible definitions.

Paul

'Christian Atheism could mean sustaining a religion with Jesus at the centre, but *without* God. In which case Jesus would have to be especially important - more so than, say, Plato - in such a way as to be almost divine. In the Christian paradigm, by virtue of his relationship to God, Jesus is in some sense divine and when this is recognised, he becomes the centre of the believer's life. If you take divinity away, what's so special about Jesus? How different is he from, say, Mill, or Bentham, or Kant? So without a divine element, surely you have got to rethink the place of worship. You can't make much sense of worshipping another human being.'

BM

I take the point. But not all worship is directed outwards to the divine. Prayers and some hymns are addressed to God, usually expressing praise or asking for some benefit, but worship also functions in a much more inward way as a ritual of community, or of ethics, or aesthetics – a beautiful service with music and words which inspire. In much worship these days, attention is directed to each other, the sharing of the Peace a classic example. An acquaintance told me that she's 'not a believer' but accompanies her partner to church out of a sense of friendship and commitment, and there she finds both the liturgy and the company congenial. It seems therefore that 'worship' can have a kind of legitimacy for some people quite apart from a belief in the divine.

Paul

'OK. Another sense of Christian Atheist could be that you take a modernist approach to language. That's to say, it isn't meant to look as it looks, and doesn't mean exactly what it seems to mean. There's a Christian story and a tradition of Christian imagery which is helpful and life-enhancing, but with no metaphysical reality behind it all.'

BM

This sounds like the *Sea of Faith* movement, led by Don Cupitt in the nineteen eighties. I think he said almost exactly what you've just stated: language *is* reality; and God, salvation, heaven, how to find fulfilment etc., are all embedded in the language of Christian story. What is curious to me is that that always seemed a sadly denuded form of religion at the time, yet is extremely close to some forms of Christian Atheism I am now encouraging Christianity to embrace. Maybe it's because *Sea of Faith* was set up as an organisation, like another denomination, requiring its own exclusive form of creedal allegiance, whereas your hangers-on are at least hanging on to a wider, richer tradition with very broad possibilities.

Paul
'There's a third description of Christian Atheism you might call
'anti-militant-atheism.' That's to say, an atheism with different
priorities from Dawkins or Hitchens; a position that doesn't
regard trying to convince people that God doesn't exist as the
most important intellectual task in our society. Under the
category of anti-militant-atheism you would be saying that
religious belief doesn't hold up anything important enough to
justify Dawkins effort in refuting it. So to people like Dawkins
and Hitchens one is inclined to say, get a life. Their militant
atheism is unattractive and extreme, in such a way that I might
be tempted to soften it by taking a halfway position.'

'Nothing returns one quicker to God than the sight of a
scientist with no imagination, no vocabulary, no sympathy, no
comprehension of metaphor, and no wit, looking soulless and
forlorn amid the wonders of nature.'[34]

*

David's last gasp, tentative grip on the cliff face of religious belief
is highlighted by the following comment:

David
'I dislike the word 'atheist' on the grounds that it defines a
positive position in negative terms. I don't want my belief system
to be parasitic on religion, merely defined by non-belief in God.
An atheist can live a virtuous and purposeful life without
reference to meaningless (to him or her) notions of the supernatural.'

So he's stopped trying to justify to himself the Christian belief he
questioned so radically in his twenties and now wants to find a
self-authenticating humanist creed. In his OUP *Very Short*

Introduction to Atheism, Julian Baggini argues that although atheism is etymologically the negative of theism, belief in God, you can't simply judge a word by its etymological roots. He cites the Italian pasta, 'tagliatelli,' literally meaning 'bootlaces.' You might equally mention 'prevent,' literally 'come before;' or the 'nave' of a church, literally meaning 'ship,' from the Latin. If there were no religion and no history of belief in divine beings, you would still be able to develop a philosophy from a humanist starting point that would take for granted the non-existence of any metaphysical being. The fact that we call this 'atheism' is neither here nor there.

Bella's view supports this without being so specific:

Bella
'Basically I'm a Christian Atheist, not through any residual allegiance to God, but because everything I know about God culturally is seen from a Christian point of view. I take that seriously and want to learn more.'

*

If David and Bella are content with atheism tempered by a bit of religion, Philip Pullman, Roger, and Nigel like their religion tempered by atheism. Nigel and I, you recall from our interview, tried to identify various subcategories of Christian atheist. There was the choir member who joked that rather than being Anglo Catholic she was Anglo Choral. It seemed to me Nigel was in this category since making music is one of the main draws of his local church for him and Roger certainly is Anglo Choral (and very tickled to be so), because he belongs to his wife's choir and likes to sing Evensong. Nigel could also be a 'Christian morality atheist' or a 'community atheist.' Then there are the Prayer Book atheists like Philip Pullman and Alan Bennett, and numinous building atheists like Philip Larkin (thinking particularly of his poem *Church Going*), and the God-in-nature or God-in-self atheists like D H Lawrence. 'It is a fine thing to establish one's own religion in one's own heart,' he wrote, 'not to be dependent on tradition and second hand ideals.' And of course all those who would prefer to be classified as agnostic, just not knowing, but often devout.

Like Philip Pullman, I'm a fan of the Book of Common Prayer, but for me it's not simply a repository of beautiful and memorable language that lifts the spirit; it provides a language of prayer that, after many years of flat modern liturgy, still comes pouring back when I feel compelled to address God. Along with the Lord's Prayer in the traditional form, the collect for the Seventh Sunday after Trinity is one of the prayers so memorable to me that I am sure I would repeat it over and over again *in extremis*.

'Lord of all power and might, who art the author and giver of all good things:
graft in our hearts the love of thy name, increase in us true religion,
nourish us with all goodness, and of thy great mercy keep us in the same;
through Jesus Christ thy Son our Lord, Amen.'

But I am not a Christian *because* of the Book of Common Prayer; it is simply that I find the language and rhythms of that book express for me something of what you might call the beauty of holiness. Far better to reflect on God through poetic, evocative prose than in strangulated, politically correct committee speak; the same difference perhaps as between a gothic cathedral and church hall. And it's significant that cathedral ministry is one of the points of church growth in Britain, suggesting that people find numinous atmosphere uplifting.

Addressing the Prayer Book Society in Blackburn, Alan Bennett[35] says he's not sure whether he believes in God, so wonders if he ought to talk about the Prayer Book at all. But he does and unwittingly makes himself a fine example of a Prayer Book atheist. Like so many writers he admires the 'poetry, mystery, (and) the beauty of the language' but suggests to the BCP addicts that this is incidental, given that the primary purpose of the Church is 'to bring people to God,' although beauty is not irrelevant or incidental in this process. It's the same point I made to Philip Pullman: that I wonder whether the effectiveness of this Prayer Book prose isn't somehow impaired for him as an atheist by having as its main purpose a communication with God through *prayer*, which he admits is an interesting intellectual problem, but not one that really worries him. 'What I get from the Book of Common Prayer is community with my ancestors,' he says. 'I've absorbed the Church's rituals and I enjoy its language, which I knew as a boy, and now that it's gone I miss it. I think the Church has abandoned the best part of what it is – the Book of Common Prayer. Just think of the prayer for the Church Militant or the General Confession: what great prose, what great language. I suppose sixteenth and seventeenth century English prose is prose at its best, reaching a peak of beauty, power and richness. By comparison the modern liturgy is very flat.'

I ask myself whether this isn't just cultural nostalgia, an abstruse form of thinking that things ain't what they used to be. The Church of Prayer Book country parsons, ministering to a single village parish, is a thing of the past, no longer remotely like it was in Pullman's 'fifties childhood, which means his is an end-of-era experience that cannot be repeated? The Church of England cannot rely on a ready supply of new Prayer Book atheists; they're inevitably a dying breed. Today's clergy grandchildren might just as likely have a clergy grandmother who teaches them the lacklustre prose of *Common Worship*.

Nevertheless, 2011 marks the quatercentenary of the King James Bible, published in 1611. By that date the Bible had been read publicly in churches in the English 'common tongue' for only eighty years, but there was already such a plethora of different translations that it was thought good to have just one. Scholars gathered in the Jerusalem Chamber at Westminster Abbey to undertake the task anew. Yet it was William Tyndale's translation of 1525 that provided the underlying inspiration for the text. His was a flowing, rhythmic, speakable style, with a strong sense of indigenous vocabulary hard to beat. It captured the spirit of English and the regular public reading of it meant that the language of the Bible and the idioms of Tyndale went to the heart of our language, just as Shakespeare was to do for more secular speech.

Melvyn Bragg suggests that by 1611 common speech no longer employed the 'ye' and 'thou' and 'gat' and 'spake' of Tyndale's day, but these words were in many cases retained, as in 'O ye of little faith.' It may have been deliberate policy to keep these archaic forms. He says, 'they made the Bible feel ancient, mysteriously spiritual, out of the past, imbued with deeply rooted traditional authority.'[36] That is, as far as I can see, exactly how the lovers of the Prayer Book and King James Bible feel, many of them literary types, who access religion not through a sense of God, but through the ancientness, mystery and rootedness of language, which is not to deny that some will be led by the numinous of words to apprehend divinity.

I guess this mind-set, with which I have the utmost sympathy, is not unlike that other annual paradox of secular society, the Christmas phenomenon, when hordes of extra people, who wouldn't otherwise darken the church door, flock to carol services to hear the Christmas story - often in the old language: Mary 'brought forth her firstborn son, and wrapped him in swaddling clothes, and laid him in a manger; because there was no room for them in the inn' – and the playing of the merry organ and sweet singing in the choir. What is the religious lure of Christmas, so compelling on 24 December yet evaporated by 1 January? Somehow the story of prophecy and expectation, culminating in the miraculous birth of an outcast messiah in conditions of abject poverty, speaks to the human sense of vulnerability and mystery. Through it people encounter the mystery in themselves, and find here a parable of hope for everyman, a light shining in the darkness. The drama of angels, shepherds, the Son of God in a cattle trough and the flight from murderous Herod awakens awe and repentance, creating a window on values that transcends the shallow materialism characteristic of the season in Western cultures. Of course there's also the strong nostalgic pull of remembered childhoods and folk tradition, such as the sentimentalised Dickensian version, but hangers-on, and once-a-yearers, and Christian Atheists pile in to the joy and delight of the clergy. When after the festive season a Bishop asks a vicar, 'Did you have a good Christmas?' he is not enquiring about the well-being of the vicar's family, but whether there had been a profusion of bums on seats.

God: noun or verb, the answer or the question? A reprise of thoughts about God

My clergy colleague, Charlotte Bannister Parker, took her sons to a weekend youth camp and, sitting round the campfire after the kids had gone to bed, six other parents, all of whom declared themselves atheists, pressed her to justify her faith and kept her talking until two in the morning. Why? If they were so sure of the boundaries between their atheism and her faith, why bother to burn the midnight oil over it? Presumably because, despite their declared views, they still thought the issue of the existence of God not a silly question.

In this penultimate chapter I want to remind myself and you, dear reader, that there is not one correct version of God – whether the 'immortal, invisible God only wise' or the 'materialist' caricature of a supersize person who randomly interferes with the lives of those who believe in him – but many, theologically legitimate, alternative ways of thinking about God, both in and outside the box. Discussing the problem of eternal life, Julian Barnes cites the response of Jules Renard to those who accused him of atheism. 'You tell me I'm an atheist because we do not each of us seek God in the same way. Or rather, you believe that you've found him. Congratulations. I'm still searching for him.'[37]

So I want to attempt to describe how God works for me. For any clergyman it's almost inevitable that much of his or her thinking is developed in the preparation of sermons. This in turn can lead to bite size thoughts, since there's never time to develop an argument in depth, unless of course you preach an extended series of sermons over many weeks, like Karl Barth did on the Epistle to the Romans. Trying to compress too much into a short address at the Christmas Midnight Mass, I got into terrible trouble with a couple of parishioners for saying the Incarnation is a metaphor. To be exact, I quoted from two Christmas carols: 'Hark the Herald Angel sings':'Veiled in flesh the godhead see/Hail the incarnate deity' and Christina Rosetti's 'Love came down at Christmas/Love all lovely love divine.' I suggested both are saying something along the lines that the God we cannot see is visible and present in Jesus Christ. But we make a mistake if we take this idea of the incarnation too literally, too much as a quasi-scientific explanation. We are not talking about the infinite reality of God being radiated like light waves or sound waves or god particles, into the baby lying in a manger, but saying something more along the lines that in Jesus we recognise what I called in the discussion of ethics a 'godwardness,' an illumination of values, a moral vision that transcends the rules and laws of our daily political intercourse.

On the night I received the usual supportive and uncritical endorsements from people, buoyed up by the Christmas spirit, as they left the church, but two months later, at a supper party, these two parishioners unleashed their disapproval. Their censure was two-pronged: by only giving my own opinion I misrepresented Christianity, which has a much wider view - a point I gladly conceded – and, secondly, that I should be faithful to the creed. 'Ah,' said Michael, 'you have defining Christian creeds, a specific, defining agenda: you should stick to it or join another organisation' – the same point, expressed in stronger terms, which Paul Snowdon had made in the chapter about doctrine.

I am not clear if my critics were more concerned about whether I was undermining the doctrine of the Trinity, which depends on Christ's divinity if it is to work, or that I was dumbing down the notion of the miraculous. Maybe I could paraphrase their argument thus: 'The Nicene Creed gives a matter of fact account of the key events of the Christian revelation; therefore you should, in your official role as a priest, support a literal interpretation of the incarnation for it to be valid.' But what can be literal about it? God cannot be defined or demonstrated and therefore the sense in which God is 'in Christ' can only be a kind of picture. Creeds only really provide a chart for navigating mystery. The same might be said of the great narratives of the Bible.

In Pullman's *Northern Lights*, Lyra is talking to her father Lord Asriel and has just read out a quotation from (her world's) Genesis. Her father then says: 'think of Adam and Eve like an imaginary number, like the square root of minus one: you can never see any concrete proof that it exists but if you include it in your equations you can calculate all manner of things that couldn't be imagined without it.'[38] That surely is a key to the mystery of faith, that symbol and metaphor are unlocking devices for mystery. The symbols are not 'the truth' but a kind of algebra for interpreting the truth.

Speaking about science's hope of finding a theory of every-thing, Martin Rees says we shouldn't assume that a unifying theory will necessarily lie within the scope of human cognition; i.e. our brains, which evolved for survival on the plains of Africa, are probably not big enough to process all the data and all the ideas that would be involved in a theory of everything. 'We are the outcome,' he says, 'of four billion years of evolution, but we're not the culmination.' Maybe the human brain will evolve further or another animal brain will evolve capable of computing even more ideas and information. At another point in the interview Rees adds, 'Absence of evidence is not evidence of absence.' He doesn't apply this maxim to God, but I do – and find it very useful.

Maybe the nub of the God problem for both believers and burners of the midnight oil hinges on whether materialism is the only way of understanding existence. If God is to be thought of as some supernatural entity understood in concrete terms, as if based on the laws of physics, you would have to give a scientific account of the supernatural in the Bible, with walking on the water requiring the local suspension of gravity and physical resurrection the reversal of all known biological processes. As we have seen, that interpretation of God is exactly the kind so categorically rejected by many of the Christian Atheist critics and indeed by a very large proportion of liberal minded Christians too. Interestingly the 'materialist' believer would not have any problem accepting *as metaphors* St Paul's great statements about putting on the whole armour of God or of Christian people as the Body of Christ. These tropes are besides embodied in the New Testament text. But are the resurrection stories of Mary Magdalene in the Garden or the Road to Emmaus very much different? Is incarnation, the 'Word that became flesh and dwelt amongst us,' very much different?

This is by no means a twenty-first century problem. The great protestant, evangelistic elaborator of biblical text, John Bunyan, who in *Pilgrim's Progress* (1678) exhorts his hero *Christian* to find God and salvation, talks in 'the Author's Apology for his Book' of the ideological tension between literalists and poets.

'But they want solidness. Speak, man, thy mind.
They drown the weak; metaphors make us blind.
Solidity, indeed, becomes the pen
Of him that writeth things divine to men:
But must I needs want solidness, because
By metaphors I speak? Were not God's laws,
His gospel laws, in olden time held forth
By types, shadows, and metaphors?

...grave Paul him nowhere doth forbid
The use of parables, in which lay hid
That gold, those pearls, and precious stones that were
Worth digging for, and that with greatest care.'

Emergent materialism

My first attempt for thinking about God is the idea of 'emergent materialism.' To understand this it's important first to recognise that materialism itself is the idea that everything is ultimately formed of physical stuff. But in teasing out religious questions, we have frequently referred to notions such as love, value, and intention – realities not susceptible to purely physical description. These realities could be said to *emerge* from the biochemistry of brains and while becoming evident in the physical process of brain activity, nevertheless being irreducibly distinct from brain chemistry. A big question is whether they could exist without brains. Critics will say that emergent materialism leads to mind/body dualism and is rather like having your cake and eating it - you want to speak the language of scientific materialism, yet deny its absolute truth. But does this line of argument work and is it consistent with experience? Can concepts, say, of justice, kindness and love (or for that matter evil) have any meaning independent of their actual realisation in human action? Many philosophers would say that they can, for example we can conceive of justice even if no one acted justly. Similarly we can conceive of perfection even though no one is perfect, which of course is the Christian view: sinful humans recognising their sinfulness aspire to an independent standard of goodness (God). In these terms it's not entirely unreasonable to think that the mind of god – the *logos* – should exist and become real in human experience: a possibility analogous to the inventor's brainwave being physically realised in the construction of her invention, or a dramatist's play, which emerges from his mind and imagination, being acted out and made real on the West End stage. In his autobiographical book *'Growing up in a War'*, the philosopher Bryan Magee says that early in his life he realised that 'a play is not its words, it is something else, something intangible, that stands behind the words – though the language is needed for us to make contact with it'.[39] This is not the argument from design: I am not proposing God as the divine Brunel or the divine Shakespeare. I'm simply trying to show that there are realities of value and meaning existent in our order independent of whether they are realised or not. It's a step on the way to explaining the God I believe in and maybe a way forward for those who have rejected God, but miss him.

Keith Ward takes up the idea of emergent materialism in his counterblast to Dawkins, *Why there almost certainly is a God*, where he says that if you are an emergent materialist, at least you have entered a landscape where some idea of God could be formed, since you admit that 'not everything is a physical object in space' and he cites contemporary philosophers and physicists, like Roger Penrose and Peter Atkins, neither of whom have a pro-religion axe to grind, who think there are, or may be, other layers of reality. In this paradigm you might say it is recognised that physical reality is not necessarily the ultimate reality and that underlying it there is a necessary realm of conceptual timeless truths, and this universe arises from it. Such an approach provides an important tool for thinking about God - not a route to proving God, of course - but certainly one that suggests ideas of God are not absurd. Hence Ward's claim for a holistic, open and emergent universe grounded in conscious, value-oriented reality.

Anyone reading this from the sceptical point of view will point out that I am straying now into confessional language, the language of faith, which is true. Faith remains faith and there's no escape from that, but I hope this doesn't simply translate as prejudice remains prejudice. I think that the least this argument calls for is open-mindedness and the recognition that as the technology for viewing our cosmological environment broadens, and as physicists are drawn into the contemplation of a multiverse, other dimensions, and nano unpredictability, so our understanding of origins and the scale of existence expands in such a way as to reveal new levels of reality.

Noun or verb

In 1995 a survey of nearly 1500 students in the Catholic University of Nijmegen were asked the question, what is the meaning of God for you?[40] Their answers revealed a range of views even amongst those who are religious.

- 30% described a relationship: God was a friend, father etc
- 19.4% gave a transcendent description: God is all powerful, all knowing, a mystery, cannot be represented
- 14.8% said God is immanent: present in everything, the power in me, justice, love, is the deepest dimension of my life
- 20.5% were vague: a feeling, an experience, everything we can't explain
- 12.6 were agnostic
- 13.6 said they were atheist (despite being at a catholic university)

Interestingly only one category uses concrete nouns for God, although at 30% it's the largest. In the history of language the most primitive words are nouns, a name given to an object, the most basic unit of speech. In that sense a noun may not be the most sophisticated way of revealing God. Yet it's an obvious route. God is *maker, lord, king, father, judge, saviour, Spirit, master* - and if not a noun then a personal pronoun, the he, you and thou of prayers. All are anthropomorphising words that objectify God, each in a sense reductionist. They emphasize the power and rule of God and hark back to primitive, pagan ideas of God, modelled on the despotic rulers of the ancient states and tribes from which they emerge. In this view God is seen as a great king directing affairs from his universal throne – the kind of super-natural God you want to reject. DH Lawrence declared that God 'isn't really quite a word. It's an ejaculation and a glyph' - a pointer, a reference, a symbol for something we do not know. To some degree both Judaism and Islam try to head off the problem by forbidding images of God: in Judaism you are not allowed even to write God's name, let alone make a graven image. Yet, for all that, much of the Old Testament portrays a tribal, partisan God, not averse to slaying the enemy or to the occasional employment of biological warfare, as in the plagues of Egypt. Of course, that picture is counter balanced by great passages such as Isaiah 53 and the Psalms where a more sophisticated view provides an imagery for the ideas of godly fellow-suffering that pervade Christian theology. Inevitably, any contemplation of the infinite will involve downsizing in order for the brain not to blow a fuse. But at its best Christianity paints a very different picture: a god of love, humility and shared suffering. Those, too, are anthropomorphising ideas, but given their abstract nature can be understood as concepts with a much broader reach.

So maybe it would be more illuminating to think of God as a verb. That besides is how God is seen in the book of Exodus. When Moses encounters God at the burning bush, he asks to know God's name and receives the answer, 'I am.' God is the verb to be: I am that I am. The name JEHOVAH occurs 6823 times in the Old Testament and makes its first appearance as early as Genesis chapter two. Jehovah derives from the Hebrew verb 'to be,' havah, similar to chavah, 'to live.' Thus in the early Judaic texts, uninfluenced by Greek philosophy, God is 'The Self-Existent One.'

Too abstruse? The god who *is* may seem very different from the empirical god who invites Thomas to put his hand into his wounded side, or who stills the storm, but not far from that other New Testament picture of the Word who was 'in the beginning with God.' Speech and existence, word and being, interlock as the basis of thought and meaning. Language is at the root of any sense of being.

The virtue of thinking of God as verb rather than noun, and particularly as the verb to be, is that God is located in the most essential nature of what we are. Several theologians have developed this idea and found it important. One of the most significant was the twentieth century German/American, Paul Tillich, who spoke of God as 'the ground of being.' By which he meant that God is the ultimate depth and meaning of being, from which, as it were, humans draw their own being – an image both poetical and philosophical. This view of God helps to answer the threat of non-being, which is one of the most deeply alienating human experiences – does my life mean anything in the grand scale of things, or am I really nothing? Far from being tosh born of 'sixties angst, this theological insight goes back to the New Testament where St Paul, on the Areopagus in Athens, challenged his audience of Greek sceptics with a line from their 'own philosophers' describing God as the one 'in whom we live and move and have our being.'

Tillich extended his idea of 'ground of being' to speak of religious faith as 'ultimate concern,' i.e. a disposition of mind that attends to the things that matter most - an idea that has occasionally been ridiculed along the following lines: since we each have different priorities, if what concerns you most is the success or failure of Tottenham Hotspur Football Club, does this make football your God? It's an easy jibe. At the other end of the scale, a Roman Catholic padre serving with the army in Afghanistan describes how, when confronted with their mortality, soldiers seek a spiritual solution – they begin to ask the deeper questions of life. Given the common experience of human vulnerability to disease, hunger, and violence, I would suggest that ultimate human concern, whoever you are and whatever your social status, has to do with birth and death and meaning and purpose, ringing out with the questions: Who am I? What's it all for? How should I act? What is right? That unceasing mental fight is the raw material of religion and it seems to me comparatively unimportant what paradigm of the world (scientific rationalism; Christian Protestantism; poetic imagination) is used to face those questions so long as they are addressed.

Philip Larkin seems to reach a similar conclusion in his often quoted poem, *Church Going*, the title itself, of course, a pun on church attendance on the one hand and the demise of religion on the other. His own position was fairly unambiguous. He once said: 'I am an atheist - an Anglican atheist, of course.' The poem describes a typical visit to a church midweek: the musty smell, wilting flowers, the 'hectoring' large print verses in the open lectern-Bible. The poet reflects it was 'not worth stopping for' and asks himself why, nevertheless, he did. He concludes:

'A serious house on serious earth it is,
In whose blent air all our compulsions meet,
Are recognized, and robed as destinies.
And that much never can be obsolete,
Since someone will forever be surprising
A hunger in himself to be more serious...'

Despite his Anglican atheism, Larkin suggests in a number of poems that he wants the church to continue its social rites and observances, if only because he believed these institutions provided social cement in a disintegrative age.[41] Maybe this craving for seriousness is what motivates the sceptical parents who kept my colleague talking around the camp fire until 2am; they are puzzled that they should share her seriousness, while not believing in her God, but in the very process of contemplating what matters find their sceptical views in tune with Charlotte's theistic views.

*

One of those who has intermittently joined my conversation about Christian Atheism, curious to compare her religious experience with mine, is Catherine Brown, an English don with a special interest in DH Lawrence. Her opening proposition takes up precisely this theme of seriousness: 'I have a religious temperament: reverence, ritual, seriousness are hugely important to me.' She emails me her lecture on *Christianity* in DH Lawrence, suggesting it will be helpful because, despite the fact he was an atheist follower of Nietzsche, his work is studded with Christian ideas and imagery. Just look at the novel titles: *The Rainbow, Aaron's Rod, The Man who Died, Apocalypse.* Here is a Christian Atheist who in 1912 was exploring the ideas I am exploring now. When I was at school, *Sons and Lovers* was an 'A' level set book. Its story of Paul Morel's falling in love with the religious farm-girl Miriam and his eventual rejection of her for the passionate divorcee, Clara, was to me, a seventeen-year-old non-conformist boy, a liberation, a sexual revolution. Now, Catherine reminds me that in that story, Paul Morel states that 'it's not religious to be religious' and 'I reckon a crow is religious when it sails across the sky. But it only does it because it feels itself carried to where it's going, not because it thinks it is being eternal.' 'In other words ontology trumps epistemology,' says Catherine. Being is more important than knowing and therefore any statement of dogma as a permanent truth must be error.

In the same lecture, delivered to Oxford undergraduates, another bit of Lawrence caught my attention, a statement of a principle that many Christian theologians, believers, agnostics and atheists alike keep returning to, that Christianity 'is a way of life, not a system of beliefs. It tells us how to act, not what we ought to believe.' Increasingly, personal experience suggests to me that this is true: God is better expressed in action than in a shrine, whether that shrine is physical or doctrinal, a cathedral or a book. Not to say that the soul isn't lifted by soaring cathedrals and numinous places of pilgrimage, but these very soon become little more than museums of religion without the life giving verbalness of God expressed through action. Even when great liturgical drama or musical performance brings a shrine to life, return to it in the cold light of morning and the vital spark has dissipated – no different from the empty theatre, concert hall or football stadium. Not quite true, I know: the sense of numinous can often seem to have been absorbed by the stones of a sacred building or to linger in the residual incense. A.N. Wilson writes that 'not only are our parish churches and cathedrals an aesthetic feast spread out across the land. They are also a subversive challenge to our contemporary viewpoint...embodiments in stone, wood and glass, of our ancestors and their way of viewing the world. A few quiet minutes in an empty church can often make our way of viewing things seem foolish or trivial compared with theirs.'

Winding up the God as verb argument, I'm inclined to go with St Paul's analogy that 'we are the body of Christ,' which I take to mean, in the broadest terms, that God's presence in the world is mediated through human action. Another way of putting this would be that salvation is living for others. Thus, godly values are likely to shine through when hospitality is shown to the stranger; when a mother forgives her son's killer; when people see that stewardship of the earth's resources means the refusal to take more than your share. Jesus' warnings of the perils of greed punctuate the gospel narrative, most famously in the trope of the camel and needle's eye – easier for a camel to get through than for a rich man to enter the kingdom of heaven. And there's the great call to self-giving, 'greater love hath no man than this, that a man lay down his life for a friend.' This is the key to the Christian moral teaching and the exemplary focus of Jesus' life. In all these ways the verbalness of God, intransitive and transitive, being and action, is underlined. In the end people are not drawn to God by any argument about materialism versus transcendence; people are drawn by generous suffering and generous love. Thus here again it is no surprise that there is a massive proximity between those parents sitting round the campfire, who desire justice and love from a humanist point of view and Charlotte who desires justice and love from a Christian point of view. They might come to see that each is talking the same language.

Poetry

Thirdly, one of the principal arguments in this book has concerned the capacity of poetry, by which I don't mean simply *poems*, but all the layers of meaning communicated and evoked by words, music, art, and symbolism, to express transcendence and the consequent recognition that for religious language poetry is of the essence. Now I would obviously want to adduce that argument again to ask the Christian Atheist whether it makes any difference to the way he or she perceives my theist position. If a major dividing line has been the perception that literalism demands belief in the impossible, this is in some sense allayed by the fact that the landscape of imagery and metaphor allows Biblical and creedal narrative to speak without constant quibbling about did this actually happen or is that literally true. It always seems curious to me that people can get so worked up about 'literal truth' in relation to the Bible and religion, but it doesn't occur to them to get agitated about Shakespeare. Who would hear Portia in *The Merchant of Venice* and insist that to understand mercy one must take her words literally?

> 'The quality of mercy is not strain'd,
> It droppeth as the gentle rain from heaven
> Upon the place beneath...
> 'Tis mightiest in the mightiest: it becomes
> The throned monarch better than his crown...
> But mercy is above this sceptred sway,
> It is enthroned in the hearts of kings,
> It is an attribute to God himself'

Once you have grasped this point, much of religious language just falls into place as the poetry it is. Here's a passage from the Anglican Eucharistic prayer, rich in imagery and imagination, packed with metaphor, but speaking about faith and hope.

Pour out your Holy Spirit as we bring before you
These gifts of your creation:
may they be for us the body and blood of your dear Son.

As we eat and drink these holy things in your presence,
form us in the likeness of Christ,
and build us into a living temple to your glory.

Bring us at the last with all the saints
to the vision of that eternal splendour
for which you have created us;
through Jesus Christ, our Lord...

People sometimes criticise this argument as reductive, on the grounds that it is saying religious language is *only* metaphor, or *merely* metaphor. Actually, I want to rescue the word metaphor as a positive concept, one that expands understanding rather than dilutes it. But in liturgy there is also a kind of halfway house between the literal and metaphorical, which grows from the fact that language changes and more importantly that it accretes meaning from regular usage, where the same prayers and creeds are repeated daily or weekly so that the words can add up to more than the sum of their parts, so that they become embedded in the community that say them, even to the point where they become the identifying mark of that community. Another word for this is, of course, tradition and it is true of secular social identity as well as religious identity. In Christianity, the most obvious instance here is the recitation of parts of the mass where ideas and statements that are in some obvious ways culturally redundant remain useful badges of identity for the present. I think specifically of the *Agnus Dei*, the Lamb of God who takes away the sins of the World; in one sense a preposterous idea, but in another an ancient image built up with ideas of reconciliation, renewal and universal harmony.

Question or Answer

In his TV history of Christianity, Diarmaid MacCulloch concludes that God is not the answer, but the question. Far from being a retreat into agnosticism, this is a profound recognition that belief in God can never be static but always fluid. Nor is it a radical statement intended to shock. In their search for a vocabulary to speak about God, theologians have always used words like *infinite, omniscient,* and *eternal* - words that necessarily locate God beyond human understanding and therefore the subject of questioning. Just as infinity is not an actual number in mathematics because if you got there, there would still be more, so, when you say God is infinite, you accept that whatever you claim about God there is always more to say.

I think part of the genius of the Gospel writers, as opposed to St Paul and subsequent doctrine makers, is that they recognise the interrogative nature both of faith and of the person of Jesus. Jesus asks his followers who people say he is. Others ask who is this that the winds and waves obey him; are you the one who is to come, or are we to wait for another? Critics ask who this is who dares to forgive sins; why he does what is not lawful on the Sabbath; whether he casts out demons by Beelzebul the prince of demons; and who is my neighbour? Would-be followers ask what they must do to inherit eternal life? We should never imagine the gospels as the real time footage of a documentary programme; they're the edited version of a story after years of reflection and theologising. So the questions are not simply the raw questions of people hearing of Christianity for the first time, but questions the early church felt compelled to keep on asking. But because we live in an age that lusts for certainty, few want to build an approach to God through questions. Just google 'Gospel questions' and you're immediately confronted by a host of sites set up by preachers setting out to provide unequivocal *answers*.

The theologian, Mark Vernon, took up the 'God-as-question' theme in an article in the *Guardian* newspaper on 26 December 2009. His piece is cited on the Richard Dawkins' website and subjected to a barrage of abusive mockery from bloggers along the lines that the idea might superficially sound deep but is in fact tosh, mystery and poetry dismissed as completely alien to the crystalline scientific intellect. More worrying still are the pictorial 'signatures' of the contributors beside their blogs: one in a Jedi mask, an older man filmed ranting, another sinisterly peering from beneath a hood, like a mad monk.

In the article Vernon reminds me that an aphorism I have often quoted in sermons, 'God is in the wound not in the bandage,' in fact comes from Dennis Potter's last TV interview, when he was dying of cancer and in such pain that he had to take swigs of morphine on screen. It's a neat summary of that big theological question why God should seek to effect salvation through the suffering of Christ on the cross rather than by divine fiat or edict, or even by military force as the more zealous disciples of Jesus wished. In the Christian tradition the drama of salvation is ironically centred on Christ's moment of god-forsakenness, when he cries out from the cross with the haunting question, 'My God, my God, why hast thou forsaken me?' – a question through which, one might argue, God incarnate reveals his own interrogative nature as a necessarily orthodox fact.

Conclusion

As I said at the beginning of this chapter, my aim here has been to say something about God that might be more amenable to the Christian Atheist, in the sense that I can see where they are coming from and can assure them that many people who adhere to belief in God are coming from the same place with the same questions. We can speak of God in the traditional language of our religion, but we are aware of its ambiguities and inadequacies. So the atheist/theist divide is often no where near as clear cut as is often supposed.

The poet Carol Ann Duffy (1955 -) captures this sense in a wonderful poem entitled *Prayer* that was once plastered all over the London Underground:

'Some days, although we cannot pray, a prayer
utters itself. So a woman will lift
her head from the sieve of her hands and stare
at the minims sung by a tree, a sudden gift.
Some nights, although we are faithless, the truth
enters our hearts, that small familiar pain;
then a man will stand stock-still, hearing his youth
in the distant Latin chanting of a train.
Pray for us now. Grade 1 piano scales
console the lodger looking out across
a Midlands town. Then dusk, and someone calls
a child's name as though they named their loss.
Darkness outside. Inside the radio's prayer -
Rockall. Malin. Dogger. Finisterre'

What should the Church's attitude be to Christian Atheists?

Or for that matter to anyone who doesn't fit the category of 'conventional believer'?

The first thing I'd say to the Church is don't be frightened and, if it doesn't sound too condescending, look for the positives. In the last twenty years or so, as globalism has established itself, the Church in the West has been challenged to adapt to social changes which undermine its old privileges. Amongst these changes the increased practice of other world religions in our cities cheek by jowl with parish churches, the deregulation of Sunday, the dramatic fall in church attendance, lack of familiarity with basic Christian texts, so that even those reading English at university need a special course in the Bible, and the onslaught of campaigning atheists and humanists trying to defeat the Church. All this can easily create a backs-to-the-wall retreat into self-protection, where even the attempts to be innovative, such as the Church of England's *Fresh Expressions* movement, are really only variations on an old tune, playing it in pubs and clubs rather than in churches.

But there are new opportunities which, to take advantage of, require stepping outside the box. How, for example, should the Church answer the potential donor to one of its great buildings who says, 'my wife and I are drawn to this place, but, as non-believers, what's in it for us?' Well, 'what's in it' ought to be open service to the community regardless of creed, welcoming schools, music makers and secular events, a place of beauty that inspires reflection, and a heritage of people who have struggled for meaning and hope through the changes of history by engaging with the Christian story. Or how should it respond to the intelligent sixteen-year-old contemplating the interior of the University Church in Oxford who tells me she's from 'a religious atheist family'? She's really surprised when I say I understand what she means, because apparently her self-description has hitherto only been met in church circles by puzzlement or disdain. Or what am I to say when my congregation tells me that the address given by the Jewish atheist novelist, Howard Jacobson, is the best sermon they've heard for a long time? What did he say that was so compelling? I do him injustice by trying to summarise, but he said humans were not all fools before science enlightened us; 'disbelief was often voiced and doubt was common – only think of Castle Doubting in *Pilgrim's Progress*.' He suggested that 'faith is a different kind of animal to a scientific proposition.' 'You could say that this is the writer's creed – that something other than the irresistible evidence, which would alone persuade a scientist, operates when we come to describe what happens in "the depths of our being". Myself I rather like the way the Old Testament sites those depths in the bowels...'[41] Arguing via Coleridge, Keats, Shakespeare and the Genesis creation story he concluded, 'However you explain it, I like the idea, wherever I encounter it, of a God forever out of reach. Whoever tells me that my failure to reach him proves his non-existence has merely closed his mind to my ongoing curiosity.'

Or how about the interviewer for the post of Rector of a famous London church who says to one of the short-listed applicants, 'I am a convinced atheist and a member of your PCC: how would you cope with that?' One of my clergy colleagues was genuinely shocked by this, to think that the enemy was within the gates. Or there's Diarmaid MacCulloch who, unsure about God, describes himself as 'a candid friend of Christianity' and one who appreciates 'the seriousness which a religious mentality brings to the mystery and misery of human existence...'[43]

The key here is of course being a candid *friend*. Each of the people I have described and each of those I have interviewed could equally have been described in those terms; well-wishers, interested parties, seekers, batting for the same side. The clergy colleague shocked by the thought of an atheist on the PCC was of course imagining a hard line opponent of religion having a voice in church government and, although Jesus commanded 'love thine enemies,' this seemed a step too far. So friendship is different from negative opposition and what wouldn't we give for candid friendship in the rest of life? On the one hand the Church proclaims a universal God; on the other it excludes most people. How crazy is that?

*

This leads to a related question: whether theology exists to serve the Church or is part of the public discourse of a pluralist society? Contrast what ordinands are taught in a theological college and the polemics of the 'God Debate' raging in bestselling books, newspaper articles and Radio 4 programmes. Recently theologians have distinguished between three strands: academic theology as a university subject alongside other subjects like maths or history; confessional theology, the theology of a church articulating its own beliefs – sometimes called ecclesial theology; and society's general interest in religion and related topics. In a sense these are false distinctions since they are blurred at the edges and from an intellectual point of view theology is interested in all of these aspects. It was an issue that cropped up in my interview with undergraduate Bella when I put to her that 'since *theology* implies thinking about God, isn't it rather an odd subject for an atheist like her to choose.' She replied:

Bella
'Yes, but you can study theology like any other subject - history, psychology, philosophy - and my interest's in the historical, literary and cultural aspects, specifically viewed from the perspective of Judaism and Christianity. In fact, you could argue that much of our course technically shouldn't be called 'theology'

at all. For example, the 'Biblical track' can be treated as the study of ancient Israel in the light of the primary biblical source. In this sense a theology degree is not the 'study of God' *per se* but the study of religion. I think that interest in religion – and for the English, interest in Christianity – is a natural concern for anyone who's curious about our origins and our contemporary culture. That's where I am.'

'Lots of my contemporaries dismiss theology as a dossy degree. You know, when I first got in to Oxford, they said, so what are you going to *change* to, as if I'd chosen theology just because there was less competition for places. But people who were initially sniffy about religion soon got excited, whether for or against. They see it's relevant in the news: fundamentalist fuelled terrorism, Jews and Muslims in the Middle East, Catholic opposition to abortion or euthanasia.'

BM
'I agree that theology should be studied with complete intellectual objectivity, regardless of the confessional opinions of the person studying it.'

Bella
'Well, one of my friends, a Roman Catholic, takes a different view and says that, since Christian theology is about doctrine being forged in the historical experience of the Church, the purest study of it can only be done from a position of faith. Perhaps this is true theology – 'God-speak.' That's why he's changed to the *Bachelor of Theology* course, which is designed for those wanting to be ordained. I respect his view, but of course I don't agree with him.'

The idea of ecclesial, confessional theology has always concerned me because it can so easily become biased theology, closed and exclusive, tantamount to a sectarian party line, implying there's a right and wrong way to understand it.

In an article for the Tablet (29 May 2010), Professor Paul Murray discusses this issue and cites Gavin D'Costa's view that prayer is important in doing theology because that's what St Anselm must have meant when he spoke of 'faith seeking understanding.' Presumably there is a difference between *faith* seeking understanding and anthropology or historical research seeking understanding. And you can see that there is because the religious believer needs to think through what they believe and will be enlightened in the process just as the listener to music learns to appreciate music more deeply by understanding the principles of harmony, modulation, major and minor, music history and so on.

*

At baptisms one of my favourite rhetorical devices is to eulogise the institution and what it has to offer those who have just joined it. Recently I was presented with baby Edith Andrews and baby Edith Lane at the same service. An old fashioned name, Edith, and I'd been waiting for years to baptise one, then two come along at once. 'Let's not forget the great heritage of the Church,' I said: 'education, church schools, hospitals, social care and welfare, faith and purpose, music and beautiful liturgy, community – where else do people today gather together regularly to meet each other, sing, and listen to live public speaking? Let's hope the Ediths grow to love and value these good things.' Afterwards, a theologian in the congregation told me he thought I'd been too kind to the Church, painting too rosy a picture. What about the downside? So we set to drawing up a summary balance sheet, a shorthand of profit and loss. In the profit column we had the Sistine Chapel, Bach's B minor Mass, Michelangelo's Pieta; we had Francis of Assisi, Mother Teresa and many works of service and social commitment. Then there was a vision of the common good; theologians like Augustine, Aquinas, Kant, Barth, and Bonhoeffer; worship which dramatises our deepest needs and aspirations (although we noted that the details of worship can become an obsession for some); we had a tradition of belief – a framework to hold on to, but noted that that could be cruelly imposed.

In the loss column we had: the Inquisition, the crusades, sex abuse, repression, a love of power and wealth, clericalism, the fundamentalist thought police - a serious charge list that provokes widespread anger in many quarters with organised religion. In the wake of the child abuse scandal in the Roman Catholic Church, just wearing a clerical collar, as I have experienced, can draw venomous remarks from people in the street.

This, of course is the theme of Philip Pullman's book, *The Good Jesus and the Scoundrel Christ*. Some people give me a hard time when I quote the work of atheists, as if this were some kind of dreadful disloyalty to the Cause. But I see theology as a conversation, not a set of givens. Within this conversation it is essential that we look at what people struggling with similar questions to us have concluded in the past, and learn from their ideas. Then as TS Eliot said, we have to work out our own salvation with diligence. Pullman reminds us what many ordinary people think about the Church and raises some important theological questions. So I think he is part of the conversation. The conversation cannot be simply in house; we know this really. We know for example that the conversation now includes what other religions have to say and that Christianity doesn't have a divine right to its own opinions. It also includes those who accept some bits of Christian teaching but not others and those who can make sense of Christianity only by excluding its metaphysical claims.

Recently in Australia there was a conference of radical Christians trying to redefine the nature of faith. They were exploring what they called 'the common space of the occasionally false dichotomy between believers and unbelievers' – a circumlocutive way of saying that the distinction between belief and disbelief is not clear cut, but between those two positions lies a big amorphous space where most people interested in religion are actually to be found. Nervous and reluctant about grey areas, this is not a fact that the Church has readily embraced, since grey areas compromise the Church's power structure, depending as it has done in much of its history on clear cut, unequivocal beliefs and rules. To muddy the waters (from my point of view at least), Jesus is attributed with two sayings that support such an attitude. In Matthew and Luke he declares that 'whoever is not with me is against me, and whoever does not gather with me scatters,' and in John he says to Thomas, 'I am the way, and the truth, and the life. No one comes to the Father except through me,' texts that are cited in support of decisive no-nonsense teaching. But in isolation these sayings take little or no account of the broader fact of the gospels that Jesus was radically inclusive, welcoming women, the sick, tax collectors and prostitutes into his society: socially marginalised people who ironically can often be more 'for me' than conventional religious types.

The key speaker was the Reverend Gretta Vosper, head of the Canadian Centre for Progressive Christianity, who has written a huge best seller, *With or Without God: Why the Way We Live is More Important than What We Believe.* She proposes that religion is a human construction once needed as part of the programme of human survival (a point made by Nigel in his interview recalling his anthropology degree), but now we know so much more than we did when faith evolved, our interpretation of religion must be modernised. Compare, for example, she suggests, the relative ignorance of a medieval bishop with the knowledge of a contemporary person, yet in religion the ignorance of the former now binds the life of the latter. We need to move on to the next stage of belief, she suggests. I agree that this is a problem for the Church that the worldview of earlier civilisations stills binds the present and people rightly rebel against that.

In Pullman's book Jesus and Christ are twins. Jesus is the uncomplicated, unselfish, generous bloke of the gospels; Christ represents the more sinister side – betrayal, complicity, moral weakness, what Eliot described in *Mr Eliot's Sunday Morning Service* as the 'sapient subtlers of the Lord.' I think Eliot loved all the high church flummery, but manages here to capture the sinister nature of it.

In my view the Pullman book has its best moment when Jesus prays to God in the Garden of Gethsemane. Here Jesus asserts his down to earth honesty, his love of life. He deprecates the philosophers – why propose perfection in other worlds when you have it here on earth in the smell of cooking, a lovely day, or physical love; the sweet taste of lips willingly offered. But this is also an extended meditation on Jesus' cry of despair on the cross – my God why hast thou forsaken me? Why does God remain silent when prayed to?

Jesus ponders what would happen if his brother Christ manages to get his organisation going... 'as soon as men who believe they're doing God's will get hold of power... it isn't long before they start drawing up lists of punishments for all kinds of innocent activities, sentencing people to be flogged or stoned in the name of God for wearing this or eating that or believing the other. And the privileged ones will build great palaces and temples to strut around in...'

By contrast the Church Jesus would like is this: 'Lord, if I thought you were listening, I'd pray for this above all: that any church set up in your name should remain poor, and powerless and modest. That is should wield no authority except love. That it should never cast anyone out... does the tree say to the sparrow 'Get out, you don't belong here?' Does the tree say to the hungry man 'This fruit doesn't belong to you?'[44]

I agree and I say to Christians everywhere: don't close your minds to all those who are finding religious meaning in ways that don't quite fit your preconceived blueprint. With some reservations I have conceded that the Church needs a defining orthodoxy, even if it's as distilled as Paul Snowden's 'God, Christ, Revelation,' although I prefer to be guided by the story, in creative dialogue with the Biblical salvation history. To the Church I say, people like us, you and me, need organised religion; we see its virtue. But beware. Avoid seeing your faith only from the inside; always be ready to stand on the outside and look in so that you can see it as other people see it. That is one of the most important theological lessons. But don't get me wrong: I'm definitely not arguing for some sort of meta-church made up of a mishmash of religions. I cannot imagine anything more ghastly and I don't know anyone who wants that. You see, it's not compromise I want but complementarity.

Would we be better off with small house churches, devoid of the clutter of cathedrals, priesthood, bishops and archaic ceremonial, or with no churches at all? Well certainly clericalism is a great enemy of true religion, driven as it is by the irrepressible professional self-interest of the clergy and their occasional doctrinal despotism - a form of corruption that also spills over into what you might call the oligarchy of the righteous: all those inner-circle committees of narrow-visioned earnest types with nothing better to do with their time. More genuine democracy is needed – the democracy of the unelected – because beyond the confines of Church hierarchy, amongst those who find the questions serious and worth asking, you find a much more open, laid-back attitude towards religion and ethics, which is essentially positive and creative. Perhaps this is enough. But is it? Is trying to live good lives sufficient? Is the occasional religious response, embedded in social and public life, enough? For some it is, but I don't think so. Institutional religion is helpful because it's strengthening to support each other, uplifting to have critical mass, inspiring to meet in large buildings of great beauty, good to organise aid and support from one community for another, liberating to think seriously about what ultimately matters, whether God, or faith, hope and love, or whatever is true, honourable, just, and pure. As in so many aspects of human social organisation, it's a case of trying to see the wood for the trees, of not allowing the institution to become more important than what it tries to embody. I am still happy for people to hang on or drop off or impact for a moment, but the church is not some solid, unchangeable rock of certitude; it is itself a living, fluid, developing, changing organism that needs for its own good health to have its DNA strengthened by less incest and more interbreeding.

So Christian Atheists are definitely part of the enterprise – tangential in some sense maybe, but contributors, voices to be listened to, thoughtful types to be taken seriously. Could it be that some of the atheists are writing the most seminal books of theology for our time, because they raise questions that resonate, they get people talking and discussing and thinking about things often left unremarked or too sacrosanct to speak of. The Church must listen to its belonging-without-believing and believing-without-belonging fringe; engage with all those who have that essentially religious temperament of wanting to think about things that matter and are ultimately important and impinge on the meaning of existence. Fling wide the doors and engage with all those who are on the fringe yet experience that 'lingering splinter in the mind... a sense of yearning for the absolute' and welcome those who want the values of religion without its metaphysics.

Notes

1 Jane Shaw. *23rd Eric Symes Abbott Memorial Lecture*, 8 may 2008, published by King's College London.

2 Charles Taylor. *A Secular Age*, Harvard University Press, 8 May 2008, p513

3 New Scientist 26 July 2008

4 Matthew 12.30

5 Alan Bennett. *Untold Stories*, Faber, 2005, p 278

6 Hans Kung. *Mozart – Traces of Transcendence*, SCM 1992, p35

7 John Cottingham. *The Spiritual Dimension*, Cambridge 2005, p136

8 Richard Dawkins. *The God Delusion*, Bantam Books 2006, p86

9 Karen Armstrong. *The Spiral Staircase*. Harper Collins 2004, p191

10 Iris Murdoch. *The Sovereignty of Good*, Routledge and Kegan Paul 1970, p64-65

11 Ibid p59

12 The Reader No 29 Spring 2008 Liverpool University Press, p51

13 The Reader No 29 Spring 2008 Liverpool University Press, p30

14 Ibid p32

15 Templeton Foundation Press 2008, p185

16 Illustration. *Blue Nude 1*, Matisse, 1952

17 See also Doctrine pp 66-70

18 Diarmaid MacCulloch. *A History of Christianty*, Allen Lane, p9

19 Tom Chatfield. *The art of prize-fighting*, Prospect January 09, p46

20 University Sermon, Oxford 2002

21 Karen Armstrong. *The Great Transformation*, Atlantic Books 2006, pxiv

22 Ibid p*xiii*

23 Philip Pullman. *The Amber Spyglass*, Scholastic Point, 2000, p471

24 The Reader No 35, Liverpool University, p14

25 Valentine Cunningham. *In the Reading Gaol* , Blackwell 1994, p396

26 Keith Ward. *Big Questions in Science and Religion*, Templeton Press 2008, p96

27 Review by Peter Bazalgette, *Prospect*, October 2008

28 Phil 2.6-8

29 Philip Pullman. *The Good Jesus and the Scoundrel Christ*, Canongate 2010, p195

30 Stephen Pinker. *Does science make belief in God obsolete?* Templeton Foundation

31 Lytton Strachey. *Eminent Victorians*

32 Mary Midgely. *Does science make belief in God obsolete?* Templeton Foundation

33 Keith Ward. *Modern Believing* Vol 51:1, Jan 2010, p22-23

34 Howard Jacobson. *The Reader* No 29, University of Liverpool, p30

35 Alan Bennett. *Writing Home*, 'Comfortable Words,' Faber and Faber, 1994

36 Melvyn Bragg. *The Adventure of English*, Hodder and Stoughton 2003, p114

37 Julian Barnes. *Nothing to be frightened of*, Jonathan Cape 2008

38 Philip Pullman. *Northern Lights*, Scholastic Press 2001, p372

39 Bryan Magee *Growing up in a War Pimlico* 2008

40 Hutsebaut & Verhoeven 1995, quoted by Michael Argyle in *Psychology and Religion*, Routledge

41 John Ezard. *Guardian*, Saturday 12 January 2002

42 Howard Jacobson. Oxford University Sermon, 13 June 2010

43 Diarmaid MacCulloch, *History of Christianity*, Allen Lane, 2010, p11

44 Philip Pullman. *The Good Man Jesus and the Scoundrel Christ*, Canongate 2010, p197 and p199

BOOKS

O is a symbol of the world, of oneness and unity. In different cultures it also means the "eye," symbolizing knowledge and insight. We aim to publish books that are accessible, constructive and that challenge accepted opinion, both that of academia and the "moral majority."

Our books are available in all good English language bookstores worldwide. If you don't see the book on the shelves ask the bookstore to order it for you, quoting the ISBN number and title. Alternatively you can order online (all major online retail sites carry our titles) or contact the distributor in the relevant country, listed on the copyright page.

See our website **www.o-books.net** for a full list of over 500 titles, growing by 100 a year.

And tune in to myspiritradio.com for our book review radio show, hosted by June-Elleni Laine, where you can listen to the authors discussing their books.

MySpiritRadio